# IN SOME SENSE THE WORK
# OF AN INDIVIDUAL
## Alfred Willis and the Tongan Anglican
## Mission 1902 - 1920

## by Stephen L. Donald

## ColCom Press
### HIBISCUS COAST, N.Z.

IN SOME SENSE THE WORK OF AN INDIVIDUAL
Alfred Willis and the Tongan Anglican Mission 1902-1920

by Stephen L. Donald

November 1994

ISBN 0-908815-48-4

Published by ColCom Press,
6 Albert Hall Drive, Red Beach,
HIBISCUS COAST, New Zealand

Subject headings:
WILLIS, ALFRED 1836-1920 | MISSIONS - TONGA | TONGA -
CHURCH HISTORY | ANGLICAN CHURCH IN TONGA - HISTORY

Cover design by Rees Morley
Cover printed by Te Rau Herald Print, Gisborne

This publication is made possible by a generous grant from
the Turanga Trust, Gisborne, New Zealand.


Cover photograph of Alfred Willis taken at 1920 Lambeth Conference,
courtesy of Lambeth Palace Library, London

Dedicated to the late Fine Tenga'ila Halapua
1910 - 1994

the first Tongan to be ordained an Anglican priest,
and assistant bishop in Tonga from 1967

# TABLE OF CONTENTS

*Photographs and maps between pages 44 & 45*

# FOREWORD BY THE BISHOP OF POLYNESIA

Stephen Donald has written this important account of the episcopate of Bishop Alfred Willis and the Anglican Mission in Tonga from 1902 to 1920. This is a valuable resource for the Diocese of Polynesia and for the Anglican Church in Tonga. The diocese is grateful to Stephen for this work. Very little substantial material has been written on the diocese and its individual parishes, which makes this volume important to us.

Stephen has appropriately dedicated this work to Bishop Halapua, who worked in the Anglican Mission in Tonga for over 50 years. Part of that time was spent working as a teacher with Canon Sang Mark, a Chinese priest who came with Bishop Willis to Tonga, and eventually took over from him.

The connections still exist today through Dean Winston Halapua and myself. My sister was adopted by Canon Sang Mark and his wife, and she eventually inherited some of the possessions of Bishop Willis and Canon Sang Mark. Some of these possessions have been given to me. The purple chasuble of Canon Sang Mark is with Dean Winston Halapua.

+ Jabez Bryce, Bishop of Polynesia
    Suva, Fiji    12th October 1994

# PREFACE AND ACKNOWLEDGEMENTS

"Of late, a mission of our Church has been opened in Tonga, but it is as yet in some sense the work of an individual" So wrote Bishop H.H. Montgomery, Secretary of the London-based Society for the Propagation of the Gospel in Foreign Parts in late 1903. *(Montgomery 1903(b):403)* He was concerned about the entry into Tonga of Alfred Willis D.D., who had recently resigned as the Anglican Bishop Of Honolulu, and who had responded to the request of the former followers of Shirley W. Baker to establish the Anglican Church in the Kingdom. Montgomery was concerned about the implications of Willis' action for both Anglican order and jurisdiction and relationships with other missionary bodies in the South Pacific. As a consequence, Baker's Church, often incorrectly referred to as the Siasi 'a Vika, and the "perplexing Bishop Alfred Willis" *(Forman 1974:4)* have received brief mention in both political and religious histories of the Pacific. *(e.g. Thomson 1902:161-163; ibid 1937:205; Garrett 1982:264, 276, 285: Forman 1982:42-43; Morrell 1973:209-213)*

This book is an attempt to examine and analyse the work of Alfred Willis in Tonga from the point of view of the Church which he established, where all power, spiritual and temporal, was concentrated in his person. Baker's Church, and Willis' experience, both in England and his thirty stormy years in the Kingdom, Republic and Territory of Hawai'i, are examined in an effort to provide background to the Willis' Tongan Mission. The Tongan Anglican Mission was one of the second wave denominations in the Kingdom. It is therefore essential to see Willis' work against the broader canvas of the dominant socio-political force in Tonga, those Churches which have their origins in the Christian gospel brought by the original Wesleyan missionaries. Religion, culture and power politics have long been closely linked in the Kingdom, and although Willis' Mission had little impact outside of its small membership, the effect of these factors was felt in the infant Church in a period of frequent political upheaval.

Willis held the grandiose view that the Church of England, as a branch of the Church true and Catholic, should become the National Church of Tonga. This elevated idea of the role of the Anglican Church, along with Willis' absolute control of the life of the Mission, caused major problems following his death in 1920. Alfred Willis' impact was felt within the Anglican Church in Tonga for several decades to follow. This is **not** a biography of Alfred Willis, as it covers only the last eighteen of his eighty four years. It is rather an analysis of Willis's influence on the Tongan Anglican Mission. Endnotes for each chapter give an indication of source materials used. Included in the selected bibliography is a list of published material produced by Willis' Mission. Much of this was collated from secondary sources, and may no longer be in existence.

Although little has been written on the work of the Anglican Church in Polynesia, two theses produced in the early 1970s at Pacific Theological College dealt with some aspects of the work of Alfred Willis in Tonga. John Pinson's "The Diocese of Polynesia 1868-1910" (1970) discussed at length the implications of Willis' entry for the formation of the Diocese of Polynesia. Viliami Tavake Tohi's "A Study of the Nature of the Church, as seen in the Anglican Church in Tonga" (1972), in addition to outlining the work of Willis from his available sources, did the valuable and difficult task of reconstructing the establishment and demise of Baker's Church, using material not available to Pinson. Tavake had the advantage of being Tongan, and conducted interviews with several people who had been party to the events of 1899 to 1901. Many of those interviewed died during and soon after he completed his research. I am indebted to Tavake for the work which forms the basis for much of chapter one. His advice and encouragement during preliminary research, whilst we were fellow students at St. John's College, Auckland in 1987, is greatly appreciated.

This work was originally written as a thesis to fulfil the requirements of a Diploma Scholar in Theology from the N.Z. Joint Board of Theological Studies. It was researched and written whilst resident at Sia-'a-toutai Theological College, Nafualu, Tongatapu from February 1988 to March 1989. Living in a Tongan Wesleyan situation, albeit in the late 1980s, gave me a feel for the dominant religio-cultural force in the Kingdom. This was helpful in understanding the differences in outlook which have existed since the time of Alfred Willis between the Wesleyan majority and the small Anglican community in Tonga. It also forced me to quickly learn the Tongan language, which was essential to be able to complete my research in that country. The whole experience enabled me, I believe, to gain an insight into the events of 1902 -1920 that documentary research alone, with field trips, however thorough, would never be able to give. I wish to express my thanks to the President of the Free Wesleyan Church of Tonga, Dr. Sione 'Amanaki Havea, the Principal of Sia-'a-toutai, Dr. Salesi Havea and his staff, workers and students, especially Koloti Ma'u, and 'Alipate Lolohea and the family at Filipai, for their fellowship and support. Malō 'aupito.

Many many people have been involved in the preparation and production of this book in various capacities; in the provision of hospitality, giving access to documents, and their recollections of the past. In particular I wish to acknowledge the assistance of the late Bishop Fine Halapua, Fr. Mataiasi & Sela 'Ahokava, Toe'umu Fineanganofo, Masiu Moala, Tia Barrett; Fr. Tevita & Lātū Koloamatangi; Fr. Siketi & 'Alisi Tonga; Bishop Jabez Bryce, Fr. Api Qilio and the staff of the Diocese of Polynesia office; Fr. Winston & Sue Halapua and the staff and students at St John's Training Centre; Margaret Patel, Robert Park, Dr. John Garrett; Dr. Sione Latukefu, Dr. Raeburn Lange and Dr. Mark Gallagher of Pacific Theological College; Ann Denton; Fr. Kenneth Perkins of the Episcopal Church in Honolulu; Irene, Helena & Paula Cooney; Pahefatogia & Vai Faitala; Rev'd Francis Foulkes, Rev'd Keith Rowe, Judith Bright, Helen Greenwood and Erice Carley; Christine Allan-Johns, all of St John's-Trinity Theological College; Rev'd Edgar Tu'inukuafe, and Rev'd Tavake and Heu Tupou.

I am grateful for the assistance of the Admissions Committee of St. John's College for the provision of the Marsh Scholarship; and to my diocesan bishop, Peter Atkins, and Colin Hopkirk, training officer, for their support and patience whilst I continued my studies; my present diocesan bishop, Murray Mills; and to the Turanga Trust for the grant which has enabled this publication.

Finally, I wish to thank:

Dr. Allan Davidson, for his encouragement whilst I was one of his students at St. John's College, and his advice during the researching and writing of my thesis, and during this revision;

Dr. Salesi Havea, my thesis supervisor, for his perceptive comments, and his ability to keep me focussed on the task at hand;

Losaline Fangia Finau at the Free Wesleyan Church office in Nuku'alofa, Eileen Barrett, Phyllis Tichinin and Kay Speedy for their proof reading and editorial assistance; Graeme Swinburne, Porangahau Anglican Parish, Maurice Alford and Brett Fitzgerald for the generous use of use of their computers and time for the revisions of this manuscript; and to Dave Mullan of ECCENT Communications and ColCom Press for seeing this book through the final stages of production.

Stephen L. Donald,
Te Hapara, Gisborne, New Zealand
11th November 1994

# GLOSSARY OF TONGAN TERMS

*fahu*   man's sister's daughter or son, the fahu having privileges over other members of the family

*faifekau*   minister

*faikava*   to prepare and drink kava together

*fakamisinale, misinale*   annual collection of funds for church work in churches of   Wesleyan origin

*fale*   house

*fale kautaha*   building where *ngatu* (tapa) is made

*hou'eiki*   chiefly class (whether titled or not)

*kai fakaafe*   feasting, in particular following a church service

*katoanga*   festival (specific use - feast where food is brought in *kato* (baskets) and divided up to be redistributed)

*lanu kilikili*   mounding of gravel on a grave

*lotu Uesiliana*   worship or church practice having its origin with the Wesleyan missionaries

*mahaki faka'auha*   destructive sickness (in particular used to refer to the influenza epidemic of 1918)

*matapule*   chief's attendant or representative

*palangi, papalangi*   European person or way of doing things

*po hiva*   church service involving mostly choir items

*setuata*   steward in Wesleyan churches

*siasi*   church (as in body of people)

*sipinga*   template or pattern

*talitali malanga*   faikava held before a church service

*tapu*   sacred, forbidden

*taula'eiki*   priest in the Old Testament and the Anglican Church

*ta'ovala*   piece of matting worn around the waist as a sign of respect

*tofi'a*   estate vested in title-holding member of the *hou'eiki*

*uike lotu*   week of prayer in Wesleyan churches

*'api*   home, allotment of land

*'api kolo*   town allotment

*'api tukuhau*   country allotment granted to poll tax payers

*'api 'uta*   country allotment

*'ulunganga*   characteristic habit or quality, cultural form

## Notes on the use of Tongan language in the text

1) Tongan words are italicised the *first time* they appear in the text

2) Prior to 1943, the following letters were commonly used as alternatives:
   b = p   g = ng   j = s
The use of the glottal stop was infrequent, as were signs to indicate long vowels and the definite accent.

3) Where Tongan appears in the text in quotation, the orthography used is that in which the text was originally written; otherwise modern standardised spellings are used.

# A PRAYER FOR THE MISSION

O God, who by Thy Holy Spirit didst put it into the
hearts of the people of Tonga to pray for a
Bishop of Thy Church to come over and help them,
to teach them Thy truth more perfectly,
and to plant amongst them a true branch of Thy Holy Church;
be present we beseech thee with Thy servant who has
gone forth in obedience to this call;
raise up for him fellow labourers,
and grant that through their ministrations
the order and discipline of Thy Church may be
established in the isles of the Sea for all generations,
enlighten the minds of those to whom they are sent so that,
freed from error or viciousness of life,
they may receive and ever hold fast
the truth of Thy Holy Word,
Through Jesus Christ our Lord,
Amen.

*Prepared by Alfred Willis for the overseas supporters
of the Tongan Mission in 1906.*

# CHAPTER 1

# ALFRED WILLIS & SHIRLEY W.BAKER

*There was no mission or branch of the Anglican Church in Tonga prior to the year 1902 (Cyclopaedia of Tonga 1907:47)*

The Kingdom of Tonga lies in the mid Pacific, an archipelego of some one hundred and fifty islands, scattered between 15 and 23 degrees south latitude, and 173 and 177 degrees longitude. There are three main groups of islands; broad, flat Tongatapu, the most populus in the south, with the neighbouring high island of `Eua; the central Ha`apai group of sandy reef islands with the volcanoes Tofua and Kao on the western fringe; steep, fiord-like Vava`u in the north; and Niuatoputapu and Nuiafo`ou, two volcanic islands to the far north of Vava'u - thirty six populated in all. These islands have been inhabited by Polynesian people for some 3000 years, who, whilst having much in common with their neighbours in Samoa, Niue and Eastern Fiji, have developed a distinct language, culture and political system.

Traditional Tongan society was extremely hierarchical, with tremendous sacred and secular power formerly concentrated in the hands of the Tu`i Tonga, who ruled as king and high priest. During the height of Tongan political power in the twelfth and thirteenth centuries, the Tongan sphere of influence extended to include Samoa, Niue, Eastern Fiji, Rotuma, Tokelau and `Uvea-Futuna. As time went on, the Tu'i Tonga line shed their secular powers to the lesser Tu`i Ha`atakalaua and Tu`i Kanokupolu. A struggle for dominance amongst the powerful chiefs in the late eighteenth century led to the assassination of Tuku`aho, the then ruling Tu`i Kanokupolu, resulting in a civil war which lasted for the first three decades of the nineteenth century.

Traditional religion was polytheistic, with a hierachy of gods common to most Polynesian peoples. Tribute was also paid to the Tu`i Tonga, considered a descendant of one of the gods of the sky and an earth mother. Pulotu, the Tongan paradise, was reserved for those of chiefly birth, with strict tapu on the actions of the common people in both sacred and secular spheres.

Spanish explorers sighted the northern islands in the sixteenth century, with visits by Abel Tasman in 1643 and James Cook in 1770. Contacts with other outsiders were few until the arrival of the ten missionaries sent by the

London Missionary Society in 1797. Ill-equipped for the task, some of their number were killed in the civil unrest into which they unwittingly arrived, most of the survivors escaping to New South Wales in 1800. The first Wesleyan Methodist missionary, Walter Lawry, arrived with his wife and family, a carpenter, a blacksmith and an interpreter from the Marquesas Islands in 1822. Their efforts to establish a permanent mission were unsuccessful, and they withdrew the following year.

Through the efforts of Takai, a Tongan from the Lau group of eastern Fiji, who had been impressed by Lawry's work, the London Missionary Society placed two Tahitian teachers, Hape and Davida at Nuku`alofa in 1826. It was through their efforts that the Wesleyans were able to re-establish their mission in 1827, having returned to Tonga the year before and set up at Hihifo.

With greater political stability, and the conversion toChristianity of key leaders, including Taufa`ahau (later Tu`i Kanokupolu and the first king of modern Tonga), evangelical Christianity of the Wesleyan variety became the dominant religious force in the country. Only a few chiefs in Tongatapu refused to become Christians in a wave of religious enthusiasm which swept the country in the late 1830s. By the early 1840s the entire land was Christian, with a significant Roman Catholic minority in central Tongatapu, their choice of denomination being motivated more by local politics than theology or church practice. Although divisions developed within Wesleyanism in the 1880s and the 1920s, the alliance of the ruling family with the Wesleyan cause ensured that Methodist polity and practice became the religious norm for Tonga.

Despite Anglican work in New Zealand from 1814, and the presence of the Melanesian Mission, and the Anglican Church in Hawai'i, there was no Anglican activity in the south eastern Pacific before 1870. A gentlemen's agreement in the 1840s between Bishop G.A. Selwyn of New Zealand and the leaders of the Wesleyan and London Missionary Societies, had confined the respective churches to their existing areas of influence. When the Rev'd William Floyd arrived as Anglican chaplain to the European community at Levuka, Fiji, in 1870, the Wesleyan missionaries, long established in Fiji, objected to his presence, considering Floyd's his appointment to be proselytising by the Anglicans. Respect for this long- standing agreement, and a shortage of funds, confined Floyd and his successors working only with the racial minorities in Fiji.

There was at least one early attempt to bring an Anglican chaplain to

Nuku'alofa. This took place in the 1870s. "all the white residents who were there wrote a petition to a certain bishop in Australia to send them a clergyman... but he [Thomas Trood] said that they did not even get answer. And when the Wesleyans heard of it they were very bitter against him" *(Y.S. Mark to A. Willis: Apia 9/7/1906)(JBP)* This effort was possibly encouraged by the success of the petition which had resulted in Floyd's appointment to Levuka.[1]

Bishop S.T. Nevill of Dunedin visited briefly in 1885 on a private trip and reported on the prospects for Anglican work in both Samoa and Tonga in his self-appointed capacity as "Correspondent for the Church in the Islands of the Pacific Ocean". The following year Bishop A.N. Suter of Nelson visited Tonga as part of an official investigation into Anglican work. He reported there to be fifteen Anglicans in Nuku'alofa but felt there would be "many who would gladly avail themselves of the ministrations of our Church were it to be regularly established" *(Suter 1886: 3-4)* Suter suggested the appointment of an Anglican chaplain, believing that the recent religious troubles had given impetus to the Roman Catholics to the detriment of the Anglican cause. Nothing became of these proposals.[2]

From 1896 to 1898, the Rev'd William Horsfall, formerly on Alfred Willis' staff in Honolulu, was headmaster of the Government College in Nuku'alofa. He exercised his ministry as an Anglican clergyman conducting at least one wedding, one funeral and nine baptisms, and the unveiling of a memorial to George Tuku'aho. Following an Easter church service, the *Fiji Times* reported that Horsfall was "eloquent and popular, and the right man in the right place when he occupies the pulpit" *(op.cit. 30/4/1898)*

This suggests that he may have held regular services in Nuku'alofa. He prepared the four candidates confirmed by Willis during his brief visit in 1897. Horsfall's work was all amongst the *palangi* residents of Nuku'alofa, with no official sanction, and ceased when he left Tonga in June 1898.[3]

When the invitation to Alfred Willis to establish the Anglican Church in the Kingdom came in late 1901, it was not from the expected quarter of the palangi residents of Nuku'alofa, but from a group of Tongans who desired the ministrations of the Church of England. To understand this call, it is necessary to outline the course of events which eventually led to their petition.

The group of people who called Willis as their minister had come together as a result of the last major public activity of the Rev'd Shirley Waldemar Baker, the enigmatic and ambitious former Wesleyan missionary and politician. Baker had played a prominent role in Tongan religious and government affairs from 1860 until his removal to New Zealand by the High Commissioner for the Western Pacific in July 1890. Baker was an opportunist, and despite his lowly origins and resultant inferiority complex, he had made a name for himself in Tonga. From early in his residence in the Kingdom he had the ear of the aging monarch George Tupou I, firstly as an unofficial adviser, and after 1880, as his premier. Baker had made many enemies, both Tongan and palangi in the process. His attempts to re-establish himself after 1897, and the opposition to his presence in the Kingdom, need to be seen in the light of his former prominence.[4]

Although Baker had built up considerable business interests in New Zealand during his residence in Tonga, including a large share holding in the Bank of New Zealand, he was not able to make a name for himself in the much larger pond of Auckland society. This was despite owning a large house in Symonds Street and worshipping at St Matthew's Anglican Church in the central city. After the nation-wide business crash of the mid 1890s, in which Baker lost over sixteen hundred pounds on selling his Bank of New Zealand shares, he looked again to Tonga to restore his fortunes, both personal and financial.[5] Baker had continued some involvement in the Kingdom despite his fall from grace, providing some of the government stores up to the time of the business crash.[6] Willis certainly believed that Baker had used some of the influence he retained to gain Horsfall the Government College appointment. He had written to the Secretary of the S.P.G. in 1894; "He [Horsfall] hopes to get a school appointment in Tonga from Mr Baker the late premier. It appears that Mr B. tried to dissuade him from coming here" *(A. Willis to Tucker: Honolulu 22/6/1894 (USPG/CLR-Honolulu 1871-1910/191)*

Baker returned to Tonga for the first time since his removal in 1890 during a measles epidemic in February 1897. The *Fiji Times*, a newspaper rarely kind to Baker, reported on 27th March 1897; "by the S.S. Ovalau [came] a plague in another form" He attempted to gain employment as Government Medical Officer, but returned disappointed to Auckland after a stay of only ten days. In October of the same year, Baker returned again to Tonga, this time with his wife. The purpose of their visit was unclear, but whilst they were there, Mrs Baker died. Baker returned to Auckland the day after her funeral, vowing to return shortly.[7]

This he did on 10th May 1898, immediately travelling on to the Annual Conference of the Free Church or *Siasi Tau'ataina* at Lifuka in Ha'apai. He sought appointment as superintendent minister of the Ha'apai district, and although he had the support of the some of the Ha'apai representatives, the general feeling, especially from Tongatapu, was against him. Before returning again to New Zealand, Baker served a claim on the Tongan government for back-payment of compensation promised by Parliament for injuries sustained by his son and daughter during the attempt to assassinate the former premier in 1887.[8]

Baker returned to Tonga again in May 1899 to settle permanently with three of his daughters in Ha'apai. He purchased the lease of a small *'api kolo* known as Fakapale at Ha'ato'u, Lifuka. His daughters established a small school and taught music. Baker resumed his work of dispensing medicine, something that he had been well known for in his missionary days. Although he had virtually severed his connections with the Siasi Tau'ataina the previous year, he travelled in August to the annual conference, that year held in Neiafu, Vava'u. In typical highhanded manner, Baker claimed that he was in charge of the Free Church now. He occupied the two cottages on the church 'api prepared for the president, the Rev'd Jabez Watkin. When Watkin arrived, he was understandably annoyed, and Baker consented to move into the second building which he had set up as his dispensary.

Baker did not appear at the conference sessions in person, instead sending a letter demanding payment of superannuation as a Tau'ataina minister for the past year. If the conference failed to agree to this, he threatened to instruct his Auckland lawyer to sue Watkin in the High Commissioner's court for back-payment of stipend for nine years. Baker explained his non-appearance at the conference in a letter, which appeared in English translation in the *Fiji Times* report on Baker's career on 6th December 1899.

"I was afraid lest my speech or words should be misconstrued (misrepresented) and someone should get into trouble, and besides it would look bad (unbecoming) for the Church to hear ministers wrangling (quarrelling) and therefore I determined to write to you" *[brackets in the newspaper report]*

However both an earlier report on the conference, published in the same newspaper on 25th September, and evidence from the minutes of the 1899 conference, show that a letter from the King had kept Baker away from the conference sessions. He did not gain what he wanted, so returned to Ha'apai by the first available boat, threatening to set up a new Church, the Church of England.[9]

Baker was as good as his word and established this new body on 17th September 1899, holding the first service in a large boatshed on his 'api. He preached his first sermon, wearing a surplice, to a congregation of between 100 and 200 people, although "doubtless many attended out of mere curiosity" *(Fiji Times 6/12/1899)*

This same newspaper report styled Baker's Church "Koe Jiaji a Vika - Queen Victoria's Church" as did Basil Thomson and most writers since the publication of Thomson's partisan account of this period of Tongan history in 1902. There is no evidence that Baker ever used this title himself. All Baker's letters and publications refer to the Church as "Koe Jiaji Igilani o Toga" (the Church of England of Tonga).[10] Baker prepared and distributed an "apologia" in Tongan addressed to the *hou'eiki* and commoners of Ha'apai, in which he explained his reasons for establishing his new Church. The first half of this document was a condemnation of Watkin's running of the Siasi Tau'ataina, particularly the mishandling of funds. The balance concerned the organisation of his Church along what he described as the lines of the original missionaries.[11]

His next move was to look to establish his Church in Nuku'alofa. Here he took advantage of the continuing unrest following the King's recent marriage to further his aims. The *Fiji Times* of 6th December noted; "Unfortunately for Tonga, just when it seems there is a fair prospect of these troubles coming to an end and of matters generally quietening down, another trouble appears on the scene who threatens ere long to be a serious disturber of the peace...it is further to be feared that Dr. Baker is desirous of taking advantage of the general state of discontent among the people for his with respect to the King's late marriage to work out his own ends"

King George Tupou II had passed over 'Ofa-ki-Vava'u of the Tu'i Ha'atakalaua line in favour of Lavinia of the Tu'i Tonga line. 'Ofa-ki-Vava'u, although of lower rank, was the popular choice of the hou'eiki and her selection would have ensured the loyalty to the King of
and Tuku'aho, who were a focus of political discontent.[12] 'Ofa-ki-Vava'u was a close relative and *fahu* to these two leading members of the hou'eiki. So unpopular was the match that the King and his new Queen were afraid in leave the Palace for some time after their marriage in June 1899. As late as 4th May 1901, the *Western Pacific Herald* correspondent, in reporting on a *katoanga* held in honour of 'Ofa-ki-Vava'u, stated, "Princess [sic] Ofa is *la creme de la creme* of Tonga society" Baker went down to Tongatapu in early November 1899 with two of his daughters and began to rally support

for his Church amongst the disaffected. It was rumoured that he had been invited to do so by Tungi, and the original intention was to hold the inaugural services at Tungi's house, notices having been sent out to that effect. The first services were in fact held at Ofa-ki-Vava'u's house, it being suggested in contemporary newspaper reports that the King had intervened. [13] The establishment of Baker's Church in Nuku'alofa apparently caused concern in official circles. The matter was discussed at Privy Council in early December 1899, and letters from both Bishop W.G. Cowie and Alfred Willis were said to have been tabled.[14] It was reported in the *Fiji Times* on 4th April 1900 that the European members of the Church of England were "indignant at the Punch and Judy Show he makes out of their Church".

There was a little financial support from the German trading community in Ha'apai and Nuku'alofa for Baker's Church.[15] Baker had remained popular with this group over the years, much to the annoyance of the British traders resident in the Kingdom.

Baker set out to organise his Church using a mixture of both *lotu Uesiliana* and Anglican practices and terms. He had made what he described as *his* translations of the *Book of Common Prayer* but these differed little from the translations made by the Wesleyan missionaries of John Wesley's adaptions from this same Anglican source. He instituted both *po hiva and uike lotu,* defending these lotu Uesiliana practices by quoting from article 34 of the Thirty Nine Articles which allowed for differences in national churches depending on local conditions. Baker used a surpliced choir, his daughters having taught new settings of the canticles, accompanying the singers on the harmonium. Baker wrote to Willis on 28th December 1899,
"We have a choir second to none in the South Seas and could your Lordship but hear them sing the Te Deum, Jubilate or the Magnificat, I am sure you would be delighted" In fact, apart from surplices, outwardly in worship little had changed from the morning and evening prayer services that Baker's older followers would have been familiar with from the Wesleyan missionaries. Baker told his Church members that they must receive episcopal confirmation in order to become proper Anglicans, and he told Willis that he had begun preparation classes soon after the establishment of his Church in Lifuka. Baker also introduced the practice of godparents at baptism.[16]

Baker had a reputation of being an effective fundraiser, having developed refined art during his time as a Wesleyan missionary. He established this practice in his new Church raising nearly five hundred pounds at his first effort in April 1900. He had already confidently commented to Willis in his first letter of 4th October 1899, "the natives are quite prepared to pay all expenses in connection with their Church"

Baker's daughters had begun their school at Fakapale soon after their return to Ha'apai in May 1899. After the establishment of his Church, this school was styled "Koliji Haabai" and described by Baker as a Church school in memory of Mrs Baker. When Baker expanded to Tongatapu, schools for boys and girls were commenced in Nuku'alofa, beginning on 26th February 1900.[17]

Baker gave his Church a constitution at their first synod held in late 1900. He published this in January 1901, purportedly pending confirmation from the bench of New Zealand bishops. In this constitution he stated that papalangi work was to be under the control of a bishop appointed by the New Zealand bench, and operate according to the canons and standing orders of the Diocese of Auckland. Tongan work was to be under the control of a commissary of the bishops, (presumably Baker himself?) in synod with his ministers and pastors. In the constitution, as in other parts of his Church, he used a mixture of Anglican and lotu Uesiliana terms. In addition to Tongan transliterations of churchwarden, priest, deacon and bishop, he used *fakakuata (quarterly meeting), kau talasiti* (membership), fakamisinale etc. Three decisions of the first synod were published with the constitution, the third prohibiting any member of Baker's Church singing in, or teaching singing to, the choir of any other denomination![18]

What became of the constitution sent to New Zealand is unknown, or whether the Church was actually organised along the lines stated is unclear. That it was promulgated in the year of Baker's demise would suggest that it was never fully implemented.

Baker was well aware of the power of the printed word and was an experienced, if at times clumsy, propagandist. During his earlier stay in Tonga he had frequently used the newspapers of his day, especially in New Zealand, to further his aims. When these had failed him, he had printed his own![19] It was therefore a natural development for him to publish his own newspaper in the Tongan language to further his Church.

*Koe Niusipepa 'oe Jiaji Igilani o Toga* first appeared in July 1900, with issues of October 1900 and January 1901 known to have been published. Baker used the paper to justify the establishment of his Church and to

Baker used the paper to justify the establishment of his Church and to present his translations of the creeds and Thirty Nine Articles. He openly criticised both the Government and Siasi Tau'ataina in his editorials and through the satirical use of animals in a column entitled "Koe Jikota" (The sikota is the white collared kingfisher). Baker described himself as a *pikoka* (peacock) and Watkin as a *kameli tuapiko* (hump backed camel). Whilst some of his criticism of the abuse of the Kingdom's constitution by King and Parliament were probably valid, as were his comments on the maladministration of the Siasi Tau'ataina, they were certainly impolitic for one considered *persona non grata* by most of those who held power in the Kingdom. Such a publication was hardly likely to advance Baker's cause. Both in his newspaper and in letters that predated the first issue, Baker claimed that he had the permission of the Primate of New Zealand, Bishop W.G. Cowie of Auckland, to "commence services in connection with the Church of England in Lifuka" *(Baker to Willis Fakapale, Lifuka 4/10/1899 )(JBP)* As early as the end of the same month, the *Fiji Times* commented on a telegram which had appeared in an Australian newspaper dated 13th October, "it is purely a *canard*; the Primate of New Zealand would hardly lend himself to such a grotesque arrangement"

This was confirmed by Watkin who was still concerned about the Primate's sponsorship of Baker's Church as late as March 1901. During a visit to Auckland that month he had been informed by Bishop Cowie that the Anglican Church had "nothing whatsoever to do with the so-called Church of England with S.W. Baker D.D. was attempting to establish in Tonga" *(Western Pacific Herald 4/5/1901)*

What is more certain were Baker's attempts to have his Church recognised by Alfred Willis. It was common knowledge that Anglicans in Tonga came under the care of the Bishop of London, and that this jurisdiction had apparently been transferred to Willis as the Bishop of Honolulu during his visit to London in 1897.[20] Baker acknowledged this in the first of a series of letters and `petitions' he sent to Willis on 4th October 1899, in which he requested confirmation for his followers and ordination of himself. He followed this with a petition from sixty four Church members from Lifuka later that month, and a similar document from his Tongatapu followers in late December. In the covering letter with the `certified copy' of the second petition (in both cases all signatures were in Baker's writing) Baker appealed to Willis' imperialism, incorrectly stating, "now that England has annexed Tonga, Tonga certainly has a claim upon the Church of England

Baker was concerned that he had not received any reply from his letters to Willis and wrote again fortnight later. He was suspicious that "others have written trying to prevent my success and influence your Lordship against me" *(ibid: 12/1/1900)(JBP)* When Willis did reply, it was not in a personal letter to Baker, but an effusive pastoral letter addressed "To the High Chieftainess Ofa, the High Chiefs and the People of Tonga". Nowhere did he mention Baker's name and Willis did not even send a copy to him. Baker angrily replied;

"I am sorry you should have sent it to her direct, as the movement commenced and is carried on by myself, and I very much doubt, apart from my personal influence, if there is a native from one end of the island to the other who has any idea of the value of the Rite of Confirmation or Episcopal Ordination" *(Baker to Willis: Nuku'alofa 2/4/1900)*

Baker also enclosed a letter in reply from 'Ofa-ki-Vava'u and others with translation into English, both in Baker's handwriting. In this the petitioners stated that they had intended their original petition to have been sent to New Zealand, not Honolulu, and that they were still awaiting a reply from that quarter. They declined Willis' offer of two or three English clergy, stating that they were not willing to collect the money. Willis simply acknowledged these letters with a curt note to Baker in mid May 1900, and it appeared that for Willis at least, the matter was closed. But as the events of late 1901 and beyond showed, this was only the beginning of Willis' relationship with the followers of Baker's Church and Tonga![21]

Already Baker had had second thoughts about attaching himself to the coat-tails of the Bishop of Honolulu, and had already written to S.T. Nevill, the Bishop of Dunedin, requesting that he visit Tonga as soon as possible. When R. Beckwith Leefe, the British Vice Consul to Tonga had interviewed Baker in late March 1900 concerning Alfred Willis' pastoral letter, Baker claimed that he had already received a letter from Nevill stating that "he intended to bring the matter of his movement before the Synod in New Zealand and that he hoped to obtain authority to come to Tonga in May" *(Leefe to Willis: Nuku'alofa 29/3/1900)(JBP)*

That Baker was changing his mind seemed to be public knowledge in Nuku'alofa. In a report prepared for the *Fiji Times* on 12th March 1900 the correspondent noted; "Mr S.W. Baker, finding his assumed position as a Church of England minister untenable, has, like the Boers, shifted his position and now styles his ecclesiastical establishment the Free Church of England. Baker, like the Boers, will take a lot of beating" *(op.cit 4/4/1900)*

Baker put word around that Bishop Nevill was to be expected by the next steamer from New Zealand, but he failed to materialize.[23] Nevill did however issue Baker with a broadly worded layreader's licence in September 1900. "...I have granted to the Rev. Shirley W. Baker my Licence and Authority to hold services in the Kingdom of Tonga, in connection with the Church of England, and to demand from the Tongan Government the lease of such land or lands as may be required for Church purposes... according to the Constitution of the Kingdom"

Whilst the licence gave Baker the authority he had been seeking, its issue was to be the seeds of his downfall. Interpreting the loose wording "to hold services...in connection with the Church of England" rather too liberally, Baker conducted a marriage between a Tonga woman member of his Church in Ha'apai and a European. Because the bridegroom was a foreigner, this marriage had to be registered in the Western Pacific High Commissioner's court. Leefe, aware of Baker's status, declared the marriage void and did not despatch the details for Suva for registration. Instead he requested that Watkin remarry the couple. No action was taken against Baker, and his followers were seemingly unaware of this indiscretion.[24] Nevill withdrew his licence in June 1901, although it is not known whether this was due to pressure from the other New Zealand bishops at General Synod, or from his knowledge of Baker's misuse of the licence.[25]

Baker's Church assembled in Nuku'alofa in mid December 1901 and prepared for their second synod. However 'Ofa-ki- Vava'u, who had suffered from tuberculosis, was severely ill and died on Saturday 14th, before the sessions had begun. Her funeral was arranged for the Monday, and Baker intended to officiate in accordance with what he said was 'Ofa's expressed wish. But Dr. McLennan, the Government Medical Officer in Nuku'alofa stated in a letter to Willis that she was "not in any condition to make an intelligent statement to anyone between the time Baker arrived from Haabai and the date of her death" *(op.cit. 20/12/1901)(JBP)*

Baker sent a letter on the morning of the funeral to the British Consulate, requesting Leefe's protection from interference, and as Baker was a British subject, holding the Agent and Consul responsible for his safety. Leefe consulted with the King and the family of 'Ofa, who indicated that they wished Watkin to take the funeral. The Agent and Consul warned Baker that he would hold him directly responsible for any disturbance that his presence may provoke, threatening him with punishment for his violation of the marriage ordinances. The funeral was conducted by Watkin and some of the marriage ordinances. The funeral was conducted by Watkin and some of the Tongan ministers of the Siasi Tau'ataina. The *Western Pacific Herald* of 3rd January 1902 reported that those who attended included Queen Lavinia, most of the hou'eiki, a large number of palangi and about eight hundred commoners. The *lanu kilikili* continued for four days and nights and ended with the arrest of twelve or fourteen mourners on the Friday for defying an order from the Premier to cease their activities. Baker and his family stayed away from what was the last major public display of sympathy for the cause of 'Ofa-ki-Vava'u.

The synod finally met on Wednesday 18th with Baker in the chair. After opening the proceedings, Baker was shocked when representatives of his Nuku'alofa congregation stood up and accused him of being a liar. They told him that they would never again come to his Church, their eyes having been opened by the events surrounding 'Ofa's funeral. They also reminded him of his frequent promises concerning the visit of Bishop Nevill, and accused him of making this up. Kilisitina Tu'ivakanō, who was present, reported that Baker, shaking with anger, replied to these accusations "Kau kai vao he Pasifiki fiematamu'a" [You - primitive people of the Pacific!] *(Tu'ivakanō n.d.:3)* The synod broke up, the representatives holding a *faikava* at Sulio Taufa's 'api where they discussed their plight.

Baker and his family packed up and returned to Ha'apai. They had nothing further to do with the Anglican Church during Baker's lifetime. He died on 17th November 1903 at Lifuka, and was buried at Ahau cemetery by the Rev'd Mr Butz, a Seventh Day Adventist missionary, assisted by a Free Church minister and one of Willis' Anglican layreaders.[26]

Word soon spread about the upset at the synod and the people of Baker's now-defunct Church were too ashamed to return to the Siasi Tau'ataina from where they had come some two years before. Acting on the advice of Tevita Polutele Kaho and Dr. McLennan, they drew up a petition of three hundred names, which they sent, with two copies in translation, to Alfred Willis in Honolulu. This petition began; "To the Lord Bishop of Honolulu. We, the undersigned, have been directed by God to join the true Church of God as we understand you represent. The Church we wish to join has been started here by someone but we have found out lately it was not true and we left him having found out that he was deceiving us but we beseech you to be kind enough and help us your children"

The balance was a pledge to provide the financial support necessary for the establishment of the Church, the petitioners stating that they did not know what had become of the funds of Baker's Church. The letter ended with the acknowledgement of the assistance of Dr. McLennan.[27]

Alfred Willis had effectively ended his involvement in Tonga with his brief reply to Baker's letter in May 1900. He was now presented with a clear plea for help, from the same group of people, but this time without Baker as their head.

Alfred Willis was born in England in 1836, the same year as Shirley Waldemar Baker. But here the similarities ended. Willis was tall and imposing, and his pedigree impeccable, being of a professional and clerical family, with considerable rural land holdings. His great grandfather, the Rev'd Francis Willis, D.D., M.D., a fellow and later vice- principal of Brasenose College, Oxford, had made his reputation (and his fortune) by his successful treatment of King George III for lunacy. Alfred Willis' grandfather was also a cleric, and his father (also Francis) a physician, running a private clinic, as Alfred's great grandfather had done, in Shillingthorpe House in the village of Braceborough near Stamford in Lincolnshire. Alfred Willis was the eldest son of at least eight children and brought up in privileged circumstances. He was educated at Uppingham Grammar School and proceeded to St John's College, Oxford, and later to Wells Theological College. He served in two parishes in the Diocese of Rochester.[28]

In 1871, the Bishopric of Honolulu fell vacant on the resignation of the first bishop, Thomas Nettleship Staley. After attempting to persuade Bishop Whipple of Minnesota to translate to the See, the Archbishop of Canterbury chose Willis, a man with a reputation as a successful parish priest, with the additional advantages of being a bachelor, and above all, a man of private means. Tradition in Honolulu was that Queen Emma had written to the Archbishop recommending a Mr Willis who had impressed her with his preaching when she had visited England. When Alfred Willis arrived in the company of one of his sisters to take up his new See on 30th June 1872, the Queen Dowager discovered that he was *not* the Mr Willis she had in mind![29]

Willis found the Anglican Church in Hawai'i much weakened by a long vacancy (Staley having been absent much of the time of his episcopate and left the Kingdom in 1870). Only three clergy remained on the staff, one of whom left soon after Willis' arrival. His nearly thirty years in Hawai'i were punctuated by frequent disputes with his clergy and laity, most of which were unresolved when he left in 1902. During his final ten years Willis was much troubled by the political events which led to the overthrow of the monarchy in 1893 and subsequent annexation of the country by the United States in 1898 after the collapse of the republic. This necessitated the transfer of the Anglican Church from the jurisdiction of the Archbishop of Canterbury to the Protestant Episcopal Church of the United States, a position that Willis found personally untenable. After protracted negotiations, he finally handed over power to Bishop Nichols of California as the representative of the Presiding Bishop, as from 1st April 1902.

The Right Reverend Alfred Willis D.D. and Mrs Emma Willis, complete with their extensive library and their household effects, set sail on the *S.S. Ventura* bound for Tutuila, American Samoa, on 28th May 1902. Their intended final destination was Nuku'alofa, the capital of the Kingdom of Tonga.

## CHAPTER ONE - SOURCE NOTES

1.Whonsbon-Aston 1970:30-34, Pinson 1972:7-10 2. Nevill 1922:89; Suter 1886:3-4 3.Anglican Church Register, Nuku'alofa (hereafter ACR) :20: Fiji Times (hereafter F.T.) 2/5/1897, 30/4/1898; Tonga Church Chronicle April 1913:3 4. See Rutherford 1972 and Lātūkefu 1974:156-220 for detailed accounts Also Lātūkefu 1975:63 for Baker's role in constitutional development. 5. Reports of Proceedings...Meetings of the Proprietors of the Bank of New Zealand showed extent of Baker's involvement. Also Trood 1912:73; Cummins 1981:324; Church Gazette of the Diocese of Auckland Feb 1899:27, June 1899:107 6. Fusitu'a & Rutherford 1977:178. Also F.T. 27/3/1897 7.This account is at variance with Rutherford 1972:173 who gives a later date of death with burial in Ha'apai. 8.F.T. 6/12/1899 9. ibid.; F.T. 7/10/1899; Koe Niusepepa oe Jiaji Igilani o Toga (hereafter Niusepepa) July 1900; Minutes of Free Church Conference 1899 (PMB 979) 10. Niusepepa July 1900; Wood 1972:203; Tohi 1972 (various); Rutherford 1972:173; Garrett 1982:276 all used the term 'Siasi 'a Vika' in reference to Baker's Church. 11. English translation in Tohi 1972:35-36 12.F.T. 20/5/1899, 17/6/1899; Fusitu'a & Rutherford 1977:179; Ellem 1981:99 13. F.T. 6/12/1899 15.Niusepepa Oct 1900 16.Correspondence of Baker to Willis: Lifuka 4/10/1899 28/12/1899 (Bishop Jabez Bryce papers, Suva - hereafter JBP) ; Niusepepa July & Oct 1900, Jan 1901; Willis 1903:2; Tohi 1972:36 18.Supplement to Niusepepa Jan 1901. Typescript English translation in National Archives of Fiji, Diocese of Polynesia Records DT/3 (hereafter NAF/DP/) 19.Rutherford 1972:113, 120-121, 146, 157-159; Lātūkefu 1975:41 20.F.T. 7/10/1899 21. Baker to Willis: Lifuka 4/10/1899, Petition 23/10/1899, 12/1/1900; Willis to 'Ofa-ki-Vava'u: Honolulu 26/2/1900; 'Ofa and others to Willis: Nuku'alofa 27/3/1900 (JBP); WIllis to Baker: Honolulu 19/5/1900 (NAF/DP/DT/3) 22.Nevill 1922:88; Leefe to Willis: Nuku'alofa 29/3/1900 (JBP) 23.Willis to Leefe: Honolulu 15/5/1900; Niusepepa July 1900; Tu'ivakanō n.d.:2 24.Tohi 1972:57; Kempthorne to Sulston: Suva 18/7/1947 (NAF/DP/DT/10) 25.Tohi 1972:56-57 using Episcopal Supervision of the Eastern Pacific as his source. Also Pinson 1970:35-38 26.Death Certificate of S.W.Baker in Western Pacific High Commission A802 (PMB 980); also Western Pacific Herald 31/1903 27.Petition to Willis: Nuku'alofa 24/12/1901 (JBP) 28.1851 Census (Public Record Office, London); Dictionary of National Biography 1964:Vol XXI p488; licences of Alfred Willis (various) and undated clipping from The Standard [1910?] letter of T.Willis (JBP); Willis family tree (courtesy of Mrs Genevera Williams, Havelock North) "The Willis Wills" (Robert Lowe, Lower Hutt); Cyclopedia of Tonga 1907:48; Dr.M.G.A.Vale, Keeper of the Records, St John's College, Oxford to writer:4/2/1988 28.Restarick 1924:136, 186; Muir 1951:328.

# CHAPTER 2

## ANSWERING THE MACEDONIAN CALL

*"The call that cometh to us from you is like that which came to the Apostle to the Gentiles from the shores of Macedonia" (Alfred Willis to the High Chieftainess Ofa, the High Chiefs and the People of Tonga: Honolulu 26th Feb 1902)*

### I

Alfred Willis was sixty six years old when he received the petition from the disillusioned followers of Shirley Baker to establish the Anglican Church in Tonga. His positive response was a natural outcome of his experiences and his theology of mission which could be traced through his thirty years as Bishop of Honolulu.

Willis was born during a period of intense public debate in and about the Church of England. The appearance out of Oxford of the *Tracts for the Times* in the 1830s changed the direction of the Anglican Church forever. The Tractarian view of the Church was that of a divinely appointed order that had been instituted by Christ and the apostles. God was revealed and imparted his grace through the sacraments of Holy Communion and Baptism, and the purity of those who ministered in her was ensured by the episcopacy and apostolic succession. The Anglican Church was part of the Church Catholic, and the Thirty Nine Articles could be interpreted in such a way as to reinforce this. By the 1850s these views had become normative Anglicanism for a significant minority of the Church of England.[1]

Alfred Willis was very much a man of his period. Although during his own years at St. John's College, Oxford (1854-1858) the leadership was evangelical and tending towards anti-Tractarian,[2] Willis absorbed the flavour of the mid nineteenth century Church. Being from a wealthy and clerical family, it is possible that the discussions of earlier years had also taken place around the dinner table at Shillingthorpe House. Wherever the initial influence came from, it was certainly reinforced by the year spent as an ordinand at Wells Theological College (1858-1859). There he was fed on a rich diet of Hooker's *Treatises on the Laws of Ecclesiastical Polity* , the writings of the Caroline divines such as Pearson, and Paley's apologetic works, all favourites of the post-Tractarian theological college movement.

This new intensified training of clergy not only developed the intellectual faculties, but in contrast to preparation provided prior to the 1830s, also included pastoral studies, missionary meetings and lessons in sacred music.[3]

All this was to stand Alfred Willis in good stead in his fourteen years of parish ministry, initially as curate at Strood (1859-1862), and later at New Brompton from 1863, where he began a new work amongst the unchurched of the Chatham dockyards. New Brompton was one of the many such new ventures made possible by the reforms to financial and parish structures which had preceded the spiritual revival in the Anglican Church in the 1830s.

In addition to the movements in the Church prior to Willis' years in parish ministry, the controversies, which were a feature of the mid nineteenth century Church, had a lasting effect on his outlook. The publication of Darwin's *Origin of the Species* in 1859, the *Essays and Reviews* controversy from 1860 onwards, and Bishop Colenso's writings on the historicity of the Pentateuch and eternal punishment in Paul's epistles, along with the brewing hysteria over ritualism, had led to much polarisation inside and outside the Church. It was seen as necessary to take a definite stand for one's cause, and there was a strong polemical argument in the writings of the proponents of the arguments and counter- arguments in the 1860s and 1870s.

It was out of this atmosphere of unresolved controversy that Willis left England for Hawai'i. His attitudes were strongly shaped by the events of the previous decade. The opinions that Willis held to his death displayed little movement from those held by his High Church anti-scientific contemporaries of the mid Victorian period.

Alfred Willis arrived in the struggling See of Honolulu in June 1872. The Anglican Church he found was described by the intrepid Victorian traveller, Isabella Bird, as "a sickly and pining exotic".[4] It had been founded in the early 1860s along the line of Pusey's ideals for missionary bishoprics and was originally styled the "Reformed Catholic Church of Hawai'i". With the encouragement of European advisers in both Hawai'i and London and with the patronage of the King, Kamehameha IV, the Church had begun in fine fashion. T.N. Staley, a committed High Churchman, arrived as the first Bishop in October 1862. His primary aim was to establish the Church true and Catholic amongst the Royal household and to cater for those Anglicans, British and American, already resident in the Kingdom. But he saw his mission to the whole Hawaiian nation, which the promoters saw as crushed under a cold Congregationalism. As the romanticism waned, support from the Hawaiian Mission Association in England died away. The Society for the Propagation of the Gospel in Foreign Parts was soon obliged to take over financial responsibility.[5]

Alfred Willis inherited and further encouraged many of the features common to the missionary bishopric movement of the nineteenth century, including, most significantly, a particular view of the episcopate. This `divine right of bishops'[6] was strongly held by Willis and led to innumerable clashes with his clergy and laity during his time in Hawai'i.

Willis followed the suggestion of the 1867 Lambeth Conference and set up a diocesan synod, giving the Honolulu Diocese a constitution in 1880 based on Selwyn's New Zealand example. But Willis resented what he saw as both clergy and lay interference with his right as a bishop to control such a body. Initially the controversy centred around Church property and was complicated by the fact that Willis purchased much of this from his own income, and desired to continue to control its use and disposal.[7]

As bitter and long-running was the dispute between Willis and some of his clergy in alliance with a group of prominent layman at the cathedral. They were predominantly American Episcopalians who had, from the arrival of Staley, found the ceremonial too high for their taste. Isabella Bird noted "The ritual is high. I am told it is above the desire of most of the island's Episcopalians, but the zeal and dis-interestedness of Bishop Willis will in time, I doubt not, win upon those who prize such qualities. Among the whites there is an undoubted field for evangelistic effort, but it is very doubtful ... whether this class can be reached by services which appeal to higher culture and instincts than it possesses" *(Bird 1874: 27, 287)* There were occasional complaints, which led eventually to a petition to the Bishop in 1881 about the conduct of services.

Matters came to a head in 1885 with a request from a large group of the cathedral congregation that they select their own minister to run services more to their liking. Willis, who had been Dean of his temporary cathedral since his arrival, responded to this challenge to his authority in his 1885 *Annual Report of the Hawaiian Mission* "until the Church is far more developed than at present, any Bishop who should cease to be also Dean of the Cathedral, might as well resign the See" *(Willis 1885:4)* Following circulation of memorial and counter-memorial, and an appeal by Willis to the King to intervene, he finally agreed to a `Second Congregation' meeting under an American, the Rev'd George Wallace. Willis himself, with the assistance of the newly ordained W.H. Barnes, maintained the much smaller but 'true' congregation.

Despite this face-saving arrangement, further disputes ensued, culminating in a petition in October 1890 from the Second Congregation and some members of the Bishop's Congregation, which called for Willis' resignation. They did so "in the firm belief that whilst your Lordship is in charge of the Diocese, peace and harmonious work cannot exist therein and the well-being and hoped-for extension of our Church in this country is impossible" *(quoted in Restarick 1924: 160-161)* Although their petition was unsuccessful, the situation worsened rather than improved. Submissions to the Archbishop of Canterbury, threats of the withdrawal of the licence of the Rev'd Alexander Mackintosh (who had succeeded Wallace as priest in charge for the Second Congregation), and litigation from both sides followed. Willis finally closed the cathedral to all worshippers in early 1902! In latter years this long- running affair ran concurrent with the establishment of St Clement's Church and the subsequent excommunication by Willis of its incumbent, Canon Osborne, and his whole congregation![8]

It was hardly surprising that Willis had a high turnover in his staff in this thirty years. A visitor in the 1880s wrote to the S.P.G. "The present Bishop lacks tact in every possible sense, he is not content to organise his forces but must constantly hamper the actions of his forces by the stupid interference with the details ... he would be Bishop but needs must see how the surplices are washed. Every minister who comes seems to become disheartened and finally goes away with a supreme feeling of contempt." *(W.T. Reynolds to Tucker: Honolulu 23/6/1886)*

Despite the bitter disputes and unpopularity of Alfred Willis, he was able to make no little progress in two areas in Hawai'i; providing a 'real' cathedral and in education.

In common with his Anglican contemporaries both in England and overseas, Willis took with him to Hawai'i a passion for 'correctness' in church building. Strongly influenced by the Ecclesiological Movement which had given physical expression to the theology of the Tractarians, Willis was determined to complete the cathedral in what was believed to be the only acceptable style 'pointed Gothic'[9] St. Andrew's Cathedral was built mostly of Bath stone and with funds raised largely in England, and was almost completed by the time Willis left Honolulu in 1902.[10] Willis considered that it would stand with "silent teaching of column, arch and high pitched roof...[to show] both Churchman and Nonconformist that the Anglican Church in Hawai'i may now be reckoned among the permanent institutions of this country" *(Willis 1887:4)*

Willis had inherited an educational institution for boys from his predecessor which he reorganised soon after his arrival and named Iolani College. He purchased a large property in 1873 on which he built his own residence and relocated this boarding school. In later years it became an important feature of his work in Hawai'i, both within the Church and the wider community. Initially his intention had been to educate Hawai'ians and part-Hawai'ians, particularly members of the Royal household.[11] By the 1880s, in response to the growing presence of Chinese immigrants to Hawai'i who had already been exposed to Christian teachings in their homeland through the work of German Lutheran missionaries, many Chinese students showed notable success at Iolani and other schools Willis established in his diocese. Many of the staff had earlier taught in the schools in New Brompton which Willis had set up, and upon which he modelled his educational system in Hawaii.[12]

The local press, who normally had a field day with the Church controversies and Willis' antics, could find no fault in Iolani College, and he was disappointed that his most important and enduring work would not be continued by the new Protestant Episcopal Church administration after his resignation in 1902. Although they declined to purchase the Iolani property, the school was quickly re-established on a new site after his departure.[13]

Alfred Willis married Emma Mary Simeon in 1883 and they lived at Iolani with the boarders of the Bishop's school. A woman some twenty years younger than her husband, Emma Willis supported the Bishop through his many disputes in Hawai'i. She was of similar social background to her husband, and from the outset she had established her standing in Honolulu society, Queen Emma giving a luau in honour of the couple's engagement in 1882.[14] Her views on the Church Catholic equated with those of her husband and members of her family served on the committee of the Hawai'ian Mission Association in London. Bishop H.B. Restarick, who succeeded Willis in Hawai'i, commented on a mission led by Emma Willis' brother, the Rev'd G.B. Simeon in Honolulu in 1885; "He was an extreme man and believed in presenting the whole Catholic faith as he understood it. His mission healed no wounds." *(op.cit.1924:203-204)*

The alignment of Anglican interests with the fortunes of the Royal family, whilst initially beneficial to the Church's interests and congenial to Alfred Willis' view of the Church and the world, was in the long run to work against its progress. Not only was there a loss of interest in the Anglican

Church by members of the Royal household, but in the troubles which rocked the country in the 1890s, Willis' strong Royalist stand did much to alienate the growing American presence and power both inside and outside the Church.

After a period of political instability, U.S. marines from the *U.S.S.Boston* intervened to keep the peace during the deposing of Queen Lilioukalani on 17th January 1893. A provisional government was installed in her stead. Willis used the pages of his *Diocesan Magazine* over the ensuing five years to advance the Royal cause, much to the chagrin of many of his Church members and Honolulu society at large. It was his firm belief that since the Anglican Church had been established at the invitation of an earlier monarch, it was now the duty of the Anglicans to support the deposed Queen. He was particularly critical of the descendants of the Congregationalist missionaries who had been amongst those who led the movement to depose the Queen. He accused them of selling out the Hawaiian people whom their fathers and grandfathers had come to evangelise. Willis considered this further evidence, both theologically and politically, of the correctness of the Anglican position.[15]

When a republic was declared in 1894 by those whom Willis described as "the Puritan pirates"*(Willis to Tucker: Honolulu 5/2/1896),*[16] Willis continued to pray for the Queen and Royal Family, against the advice of most of his Church members, including many native Hawaiians. He was also critical of the suspension of *habeas corpus* by President Dole, and was in danger in being arrested by the Republican authorities. Having long suffered the outpourings of Alfred Willis' pen, they wisely left him alone, judging that to take any action would be more trouble than it was worth. When the United States annexed the country in October 1898, Willis however quietly announced in the *Diocesan Magazine* the substitution of prayers for the President and his family in the *Hawaiian Prayer Book*, and ceased his public support for the Royalist cause.[17]

The one advantage Willis saw in the political troubles of the 1890s was the disaffection of a large number of native Hawai'ians from the Congregational Church due to its alignment with opposition to the Royal Family. Willis saw this as divine intervention, although it was the Mormons rather than the Anglicans who made large advances amongst the Hawai'ian population. One coup d'etat in Willis' eyes was the defection from the Congregational Church of Queen Lilioukalani herself to the Anglicans in 1896. He administered hypothetical baptism followed by confirmation, and she remained a faithful member of the Church during Willis' remaining years in Hawaii.[18]

The promoters and founders of the See of Honolulu had seen Honolulu as the Anglican Church's advance outpost in the Pacific. Bishop Samuel Wilberforce, in his foreword to Manley Hopkin's *Hawai'i the past, present and future of its Island Kingdom* had envisioned the Bishops of Melanesia and Honolulu advancing towards each other across the broad Pacific Ocean conquering island after island for the Catholic Church of Christ. Before Willis' departure for Honolulu in 1872, he had met with Bishop G.A. Selwyn at Lichfield in the company of the newly-consecrated Bishop of Dunedin, S.T. Nevill.[19] Although in his twenty six years as Bishop of New Zealand, Selwyn had observed comity with the missions of other Churches in the Pacific, both Willis and Nevill believed otherwise. Selwyn, said Willis, writing to the *Church Times* some thirty years later "recognised no limitations, no compacts, no fences thrown across her [the Church's] path in the Pacific"*("The Church in the South Seas" op.cit. 19/2/1904:248)*

Bishop Staley had visited the Anglican chaplaincies in South America at the expense of the S.P.G. and the request of the Bishop of London, who was responsible for all Anglicans outside of a duly constituted diocese. Similarly, Willis received a licence from the Bishop of London to act episcopally on his behalf in the *North* Pacific outside the Diocese of Melanesia or any other diocese. Apart from a few tiny Micronesian islands, there were few other inhabited areas in which he could exercise this jurisdiction.[20]

At his first synod in 1880, Willis suggested the union of the Diocese of Honolulu with the Province of New Zealand as a first step to enable the vision of the founders to be realised. This was adopted and there was much correspondence between Willis, the Archbishop of Canterbury and some of the New Zealand bishops. The matter was discussed again at the 1884 and 1887 Honolulu synods, but the idea had to be dropped as the insufficient accumulation of an endowment in Honolulu was considered a stumbling block by the New Zealand Church.[21]

Alfred Willis' first real opportunity to extend the Church beyond Hawai'i came in 1897 when he visited Samoa and Tonga to administer confirmation. Who exactly the invitation came from, and under whose authority he acted, is unclear. There was no evidence of Willis receiving a new licence for the *South* Pacific; he conveniently ignored the detailed wording of the 1873 licence. The London office of the S.P.G. apparently believed that his licence was valid for the work, although Willis did not inform them of his intentions to visit the South Pacific until he was already in Apia.[22]

The Bishop and Mrs Willis were en route to the Lambeth Conference, where Willis had a useful platform to air both his findings and his vision for the area. In Samoa he had found a large group of English people whom he believed were anxious to establish the Church of England in Apia. Willis confirmed eleven candidates prepared by the British Consul, T.B. Cusack-Smith, nine of them being the children of English men by their Samoan wives.

On the strength of this brief contact, Willis issued an appeal for the Church in Samoa with the endorsement of the Bishop of London whilst still in England. The Bishop of London also updated Willis' commission, conveniently striking out the offending *North!*[23] In the printed pamphlet which he circulated, Willis slated the Anglican Church for its neglect of the island east of Fiji. Although he acknowledged the work of the London Missionary Society and the Wesleyans in bringing the Christian gospel to the Polynesia, he believed that the time was ripe for "the fuller Christianity and the more perfect organisation that is our inheritance as a branch of the Catholic Church" *(Willis 1897:2)* Among the evidences of the "disintegration" of the missions of the Nonconformists, he cited the secession of the Free Church from the Australasian Wesleyan Conference in Tonga. In an appeal to the imperialism of his British readers, he noted that it was the French Roman Catholics and not the Anglicans who were gaining converts amongst the lapsed Nonconformists.

Willis appealed for funds to support an Anglican clergyman in Apia, fearing that if adequate ministry were not quickly provided for the local Anglican community, they would be driven to "seek the sacraments at the hands of the Lutheran pastor to the Germans or of the French Catholic priests" *(ibid)* He further believed that the influence of the Anglican Church would be rapidly spread amongst native Samoans due to so many of the local Anglicans having Samoan wives.

Willis continued to campaign to establish the Church in Samoa for the following two years, receiving the gift of some land in Samoa for a church building, on condition that it be built within five years. In 1899 he applied for a grant from the S.P.G. for the support of the Rev'd William Horsfall who have lately resigned from his position at the Government College in Tonga, and was now willing to go to Apia. Willis stated in his supporting letter that he had good reason to believe that once established in Samoa, the Church would soon spread to Tonga. The S.P.G. not only considered the work too small to be bothered with, but also were concerned about possible conflict with the London Missionary Society and the Wesleyans, who were both active in Samoa. Rebuffed by the S.P .G., Willis pursued the matter no further with the Society.[24]

The Willises spent three weeks in Apia en route to Tonga in 1902, but there is no evidence that Willis made any effort to establish the Church. This was probably influenced in part at least, by the political changes in Samoa under the 1899 Treaty, which resulted in the annexation of Western Samoa by Germany. Under this Treaty, the British Consulate had been downgraded, and Willis' Church and social contact the British Consul, T.B. Cusack-Smith had been replaced by Thomas Trood, a local trader, as Acting Vice Consul, a position he held for the entire period of German colonial rule. Trood was as catholic as Willis was Catholic, "As I incline towards Quakerism ... my sympathies are of a cosmopolitan nature" *(Trood 1922:47)*

Willis was soon embroiled in the complication for the Anglican Church in Hawai'i as a consequence of United States annexation in 1898. On 9th April 1899, Willis addressed the clergy and laity of the Diocese of Honolulu in St Andrew's Cathedral, for the first time publicly acknowledging that a new order was soon to come to the Church in Hawai'i in the form of the Protestant Episcopal Church of the United States. He told those gathered that he had forwarded a recommendation to the Archbishop of Canterbury that control be transferred to the American Church as soon as they desired it and were willing to make provision for its support. As regards his own situation, Willis intended to remain until such time as the U.S. House of Bishops was ready to consecrate his successor. It was unclear to Willis whether the transfer would take place that year or would need to wait until the General Convention in 1901.[25] The next day the *Pacific Commercial Advertiser,* never a friend to Willis, headlined with glee; "BISHOP RESIGNS ... FOR THE WELL-BEING OF THE CHURCH; CHANGED POLITICAL CONDITIONS RENDER THE COURSE DESIRABLE- A BRIGHT AND HARMONIOUS FUTURE" and proceeded to print the text of Willis' address.

Publicly there did not appear to be any other course for Willis but to eventually resign, although his cousin William Lowe wrote from London that month questioning his course of action. "I take it that the American Church is undoubtedly a branch of the Catholic Church, notwithstanding the inappropriate name of Protestant Episcopal ... I know your political sentiments are very anti-American but on matters of doctrine and ritual, are you not in sympathy with the American Church?" *(op.cit.:Temple E.C 19/4/1899)* Willis was however reconciled to the idea that his days in Honolulu were numbered, and despite his rebuff over Samoa from the S.P.G. continued his interest in the South Pacific. William Floyd, the Vicar of Levuka, Fiji, was willing to accept and in fact welcomed Willis' involvement. He applied to Willis for a layreader's licence in 1898, and in 1899 Floyd requested the Bishop's presence for the laying of the foundation stone of his new church to be built to celebrate the diamond jubilee of Queen Victoria's reign. Combining this trip with a return visit to Samoa, the Willises visited Fiji for two weeks in August 1899. Willis held confirmations in both Levuka and Suva and they were toasted by the Governor in Suva before their return to Honolulu.[26]

On his return from this second South Pacific visit in two years, Willis began to make preparations in earnest for the transfer of the Diocese of Honolulu to the American Church. He was opposed to any moves to make Hawai'i part of the Diocese of California, and concerned by the notification from the S.P.G. that they were unable to continue their grant to Honolulu now that the country had been annexed by the United States. The synod held in November adopted provisions, suggested by Willis, that would bring their structures in to line with those of the American Church, in order to facilitate the future union. This dampened somewhat the fire of Willis' critics, who had continually accused him of stalling the transfer. His main concern was to preserve Hawai'i as a separate bishopric in accordance with his understanding of the episcopat[e.27]

Alfred Willis had received the first of Shirley Baker's letters requesting the recognition of his newly-formed Church at the time of the November synod. This was followed by the `petitions' from Ha'apai and Nuku'alofa. Willis was soon making his own enquiries from R. Beckwith Leefe, the British Vice Consul in Tonga, and Dr. McLennan, the Government Medical Officer and former associate of Willis in Honolulu.[28]

It was largely on the basis of their information that he decided to ignore Baker when he replied to the letters and `petitions'. Willis' response, written on 26th February 1900 was direct to 'Ofa-ki-Vava'u and her followers. It began;
"We Alfred, by divine permission, Bishop of the Anglican Branch of the Catholic Church in Honolulu and called to exercise the ministrations of our office wherever they may be desired in the Pacific Ocean..."[29] Willis then thanked God for their petitions and felt that the desire for the ministrations

of the Anglican Church was not limited to those who had signed, but to the whole Tongan nation. He hoped to establish the Church Catholic as the Mother Church of Tonga, and in doing so he believed he would be able to heal the religious divisions in the Kingdom. Willis credited the desire to become Anglicans as the work of the Holy Spirit and likened their call to him to that of the Macedonians to the apostle Paul in Acts 16:10.

He outlined the practical steps which he felt were necessary to firmly establish the Church in Tonga. These included the appointment of two or three English priests and provision for their financial support, and the preparation by the people to receive confirmation. He also indicated that Nuku'alofa could be a suitable seat for a future South Pacific diocese.

This effusive pastoral letter had echoes of the foundation of the Reformed Catholic Church in Hawai'i in its notion of sponsorship by one of the leading citizens and the expectation that Anglican Church would soon become the National Church. Similarly, as with Hawai'i, and Willis' recent attempts to establish the Church in Samoa, he assumed that although the gospel had been introduced by Protestant missionaries, the time was now ripe to consummate their inadequate form of Christianity with the threefold order of ministry in apostolic succession, and the rite of episcopal confirmation.

Willis had learned a little from the mistakes made in Hawai'i and his abortive attempt to establish the Church in Samoa. He insisted on self-support of the work from the outset, determined not to be subject to the whims of the S.P.G. or the changing fads or fashions of private missionary subscription in England. Nowhere did he indicate that he intended to settle in Tonga, and his references to Nuku'alofa as a future seat of a diocese were vague and non-committal.

Willis' letter had brought a quick response from Baker. He now had changed his mind and was seeking favours from New Zealand, and seemingly already had the Bishop of Dunedin in hand.

Willis was pleased with Baker's response to his pastoral letter, as it indicated to him that Baker's intention was not to bring people to the Church of England, but, as Willis wrote to Leefe; "to found a sect using the Prayer Book of which he is to be the head" *(op.cit.:Honolulu 18/5/1900 - draft)* t enabled Willis to dispose of the distraction of Baker which was, in his eyes, confusing the real issue. That was, as he saw it, the desire of a sizeable section of the Tongan population to become Anglicans. Furthermore, he felt that if the Church was to have a presence in Tonga, it was best to be connected to New Zealand, and therefore welcomed the involvement of his associate the Bishop of Dunedin.

Willis saw as his biggest gain the opening of lines of communication with the King, George Tupou II. Leefe had taken a copy of Willis' letter to the Palace following his interviews with 'Ofa-ki-Vava'u and Baker.[30] This brought a prompt response in the form of a letter to Willis from the King.

His Majesty wrote stating that whilst Willis was welcome to come to Tonga and establish the Anglican Church, he warned him against doing so at the invitation of Baker or "the disorderly folk" Baker had gathered together in his movement. Outlining at length the troubles surrounding the 1885 secession from the Australasian Wesleyan Conference and the 1887 assassination attempt on Baker, the King feared that similar problems could arise again with Baker's present attempt to re-establish himself in Tonga. He also stressed that Baker's Church was not supported by the nobles and chiefs (with the exception of 'Ofa-ki-Vava'u) or a significant number of people in the Kingdom.[31]

Willis interpreted the King's reply to his pastoral as encouragement to establish the Anglican Church in Tonga. It reinforced his notion that Baker was the bad leader of a good and spontaneous movement towards the fuller Christianity which Willis represented. He then began to postulate on ways that the Anglican Church could become the National Church of Tonga by reuniting the Siasi Tau'ataina and the Wesleyan Mission under its umbrella. Believing that Baker could be dealt with by a second deportation, and Watkin, whom Willis had no desire to ordain as an Anglican priest, with generous pension, he left the initiative with the King and hou'eiki to invite him to establish the Anglican Church in Tonga.[32]

Willis' understanding of the relationships between the two branches of lotu Uesiliana in Tonga, and the subsequent political implications, was noticeably slight. He interpreted all the events of the previous twenty years from his Anglo- centric point of view. This simplistic approach was to prove unhelpful when he moved to Nuku'alofa some two years later. Baker's move towards New Zealand, and Willis' curt acknowledgement of this in May 1900 effectively ended his public involvement with Baker's Church. Willis however kept up correspondence with those whom he had consulted in Tonga and England in early 1900. He continued to speculate about future Anglican moves in the South Pacific, but his time was taken up by the faurther complications surrounding the transfer of the Hawaiian Church to American jurisdiction.[33]

In May 1900, Willis received notice from the S.P.G. that their support for his Honolulu diocese would cease at the end of June, as they had warned in the previous year. Willis' energies were consumed for several months in attempts to have this grant renewed. When this failed, he initiated an emergency fund so as to continue the work in Hawai'i until the transfer was completed. Willis travelled to the General Convention of the Protestant Episcopal Church held in San Francisco in October 1901 to finalise these arrangements. He called a synod in Honolulu in early December to confirm that the legal transfer to the American Church would take place on 15th January 1902. Willis advised the Archbishop of Canterbury that his resignation would take effect from 1st April[34]

It was against this background that Alfred Willis received the petition from Baker's former followers in early January 1902. Whilst it could be seen that Willis' response to use the opportunity to extend the Church Catholic to the South Pacific fitted with his experience of over forty years ministry, there were also personal factors at work.

Although he was nearly sixty six years old, Willis was living in a period when bishops in the Anglican Church normally held the reins of power until their death, the Presiding Bishop of the Protestant Episcopal Church at that time for example being ninety years old![35] Willis accepted that his work in Honolulu was definitely coming to an end. It was unlikely that he would have considered this the finish of his working days. He would be seeking fresh fields of endeavour in which to exercise his episcopal functions. As he told a *Pacific Commercial Advertiser* reporter 19th April 1902; "once a Bishop, always a Bishop you know."

It could be expected that Alfred Willis would have looked to his home country in which to spend his twilight years, but circumstances would suggest otherwise.

Firstly, there is no indication of any of offers of work in England in this period. Whether his reputation was such that none would be forthcoming would be pure speculation.

Secondly, the England the Willises to which would have returned was vastly changed from that which he had left in 1872. Secularism had taken its toll on the Church, and the clergy were no longer the only, or best, educated residents in the average parish. Even Willis' own class, the backbone of the Church of England, were less interested in matters religious than previously. In addition, the traditional alignment of Church and State which had been seen as the preserver of the status quo, and which Willis had relied on in the

Kingdom of Hawai'i, was now seen as a hindrance by many in the Church of England. This was due to Parliament having become increasingly non-Anglican in its composition since the 1832 reforms. The power of a non-Anglican Parliament to make decisions affecting the Church of England was particularly resented by the Catholic wing of the Church.

Although socially the Willises would have retained status, in comparison with Honolulu, where Willis was THE Bishop, England would not have held the same social advantages, real or imagined. Having been big fish in the very small pond of Honolulu society for thirty years, the relative obscurity of England would have held little attraction. Willis informed a *Pacific Commercial Advertiser* reporter in April that they did not intend to remain in Honolulu, and if their move to Tonga did not work out, they would be travelling on to New Zealand.[36]

Whereas England no longer held attractions for Alfred Willis, Tonga did. He saw a clear call to this last remaining island Kingdom in the Pacific, and the opportunity to establish the Church true and Catholic, free from the interference that he had experienced in Hawai'i from both the local Europeans and the Church authorities in England. Willis had been impressed by his brief visit in 1897, describing to a newspaper reporter in 1902; "The principal town is not a large place, but the residences are neat, the premises are well kept, and there are some beautiful lawns." *(ibid. 11/3/1902)* Willis saw a place for himself as an Anglican bishop in the stratified social structure which had enabled the consolidation of power of the Tongan monarchy in the nineteenth century.

This begs the question of Willis' decision to establish the Anglican Church despite not having received a direct invitation from the King and the hou'eiki, something which less than two years previously he had considered as an essential prerequisite to any Anglican moves in Tonga. Despite his reputation for being one for following the letter of canon law and convention, Willis also had an ability to flout these when convenient. His initial visit to the South Pacific in 1897 was not only on a commission for the North Pacific from the Bishop of London, but had expired in 1885 on the death of Bishop John Jackson who had issued it. In the same manner, Willis was now able to ignore the fact that the invitation to Tonga did not come from the King and hou'eiki, but from a group of disaffected followers of Baker. Perhaps Willis was influenced by the fact that the letter and petition written by Polutele Kaho in December 1901 was on the King's headed notepaper?

It was common knowledge in Honolulu by early 1902 that the Willises intended to go to Tonga, despite the Bishop's public denials that this was so. He had in fact received the proof of a steel die in late April 1902, suggesting that he was making arrangements for his new episcopal seal.[37] But Willis did not signal his intentions to the S.P.G. or the Church authorities in England, as he was well aware of their attitude to his involvement in further work in the Pacific.[38] He waited until on board *S.S. Ventura* bound for Tutuila, American Samoa some days out from Honolulu before he wrote to the Archbishop of Canterbury telling him of his intention to establish the Church of England in Tonga. As he understood that the Bishop of London intended to transfer the jurisdiction of the islands of the South Pacific to the New Zealand Church, he would be applying to the Primate of New Zealand for recognition as Missionary Bishop in Tonga.[39]

## II

Willis knew little about the group which had called him to Tonga. His communications with Baker had ceased in May 1900, and although Willis with corresponded with others apart from the petitioners before and after early 1902, they gave little detail of the life of the congregations of Baker's now defunct Church. As with the earlier communications with Baker, they had given little more than lists of names.

Baker's original base was the building on his 'api kolo at Fakapale, Ha'ato'u, Lifuka, where his Church had been established on 17th September, 1899. By July 1900, the Church was shown as having congregations in Ha'apai at Hihifo, Lifuka; in the village of Lotofoa on Foa; and Mo'unga-one, an island some twelve miles across open sea west of Lifuka. Lape, a small island in the southern part of Vava'u, was shown as having a congregation.[40] In the case of both Lotofoa and Mo'unga-one, there was evidence of at least some interest in late October 1899, with one person from each of these places 'signing' the 'petition' to Willis.[41] According to Baker's own accounts, he had begun services in Kolofo'ou, Nuku'alofa, on 12th November 1899, and by April 1900 there were also small congregations listed at Mu'a and Hihifo on Tongatapu.[42]

Those who had joined Baker's Church were formerly members of the Siasi Tau'ataina. The reasons for this were rooted in the secession of the Siasi Tau'ataina from the Australasian Wesleyan Conference in 1885 and the events which had followed. Ha'apai and Vava'u had been relatively free of the disturbances which had followed King George Tupou I's proclamation of the Siasi Uesiliana Tau'ataina 'o Tonga (commonly called the Siasi Tau'ataina or the Free Church) in Vava'u on 14th January 1885 following Baker's unilateral action in inauguration the Church in Lifuka on 5th January. These northern island groups were the traditional power base of the King and could be expected to obey his proclamation. Very few people in fact remained with the Wesleyan Mission (known as the *Siasi Fakaongo*). Baker drew the membership of his new Church in 1899 from these strongly Tau'ataina areas.

The majority of those who joined Baker's Church in Tongatapu came from Kolofo'ou (the new town). This portion of Nuku'alofa had grown up in the latter half of the nineteenth century after the King had established his capital in the late 1840s as his power base on Tongatapu. Kolofo'ou was largely populated by those who had supported King George Tupou I, including some families who had settled in Tongatapu from Ha'apai and Vava'u, and was therefore strongly Tau'ataina. Having suffered at the hands of Baker during the 1880s, the membership of the Siasi Fakaongo were hardly likely to follow Baker.[43]

Although Baker's Fakapale 'api was in Ha'ato'u, a predominantly Roman Catholic village, most of his support came from Hihifo, which was contiguous with Ha'ato'u. Why the people there followed Baker is unclear, but there were two likely reasons.

Firstly, some of the Ha'apai delegates had supported Baker's efforts to gain the appointment as district superintendent of Ha'apai at the 1898 conference of the Siasi Tau'ataina.

Secondly, despite official feeling towards Baker, he and his family were well liked in Lifuka, Baker having served as a missionary in that part of the Kingdom early in his career. They were noted for their generosity and charity, for their medical knowledge, and for their music and teaching abilities.[44] Probably a combination of these factors influenced the decision to join Baker's Church.

One significant Tau'ataina figure had joined Baker's Church at the outset. 'Osaiasi Malupo had been a lay delegate at the 1899 conference in Neiafu, and was accepted as *faifekau akoako* (minister in training) that year. He had been stationed in his new capacity to Nuiafo'ou, an isolated island in the far north of the country, by the conference. His decision to throw in his lot with Baker may have been influenced by the appointment to Nuiafo'ou! 'Osaiasi headed the list of contributors at the 1900 misinale which Baker had held in Lifuka, but his name did not appear connected with any further Church activities. The minutes of the 1902 conference of the Siasi Tau'ataina again showed him as a lay representative for Ha'apai. As he followed Baker into his Church, he presumably followed him out again, along with a large number of other people. All of those who followed Baker were commoners, and only a small number, eleven out of the sixty four who `signed' the 1899 `petition', were later received into the Anglican Church by Willis.[45]

The acknowledged leader of the Hihifo congregation by 1902 was Talaiasi Tuli (sometimes written as Tulimafua) who was a policeman on Lifuka. His name appeared on Baker's `petition' and he was among those from the islands who travelled to meet Willis in June 1902.

Only a small group followed Baker at Lotofoa. Sionatane Toutai had been an original `petitioner' to Willis in 1899, and had contributed to the 1900 misinale, being listed along with the choir. Sione Taufa, who was from Hihifo had emerged as the leader by 1902, and also travelled to meet with Willis in Nuku'alofa.[46]

Baker's congregation at Mo'unga-one showed a different picture from that of Hihifo and Lotofoa, both in the rank of those who became members, and the numbers remaining following Baker's exit. Uikilifi Niu had signed the `petition', and he, along with Kavauhi, a *matapule*, and Kavamo'unga-one, a *tauhi fonua*, contributed to the 1900 misinale. Others included Isileli Talo, Siosaia Hausia and 'Asaeli Mafi (who all later showed prominence in Anglican affairs on the island), as did three students from Mo'unga-one at Kolisi Ha'apai; Setaleki Toafa, Paula 'Ahoatu and Saletili Atu. A choir, which had been trained by Charlotte Baker, also contributed to the 1900 misinale.[47]

The involvement of the people on Lape in Baker's Church was closely linked to that of their relations on Mo'unga-one, as there were strong family ties between these two islands which are separated by some sixty miles of open ocean. The Lape congregation contributed to the 1900 misinale with a sum similar to that from Mo'unga-one, suggested comparable membership size.[48] The entire population of Lape's only village followed their matapule Siliveinusi Lokoeli Lavulavu into Baker's Church. Lavulavu had matriculated from Dr. Moulton's Tupou College in 1888, but had been a member of the Siasi Tau'ataina rather than continuing his involvement with his mentor's Wesleyan Mission. The people of Lape all became Anglicans upon the arrival of Willis.[49]

Those who followed Baker on Tongatapu had much clearer motives. His exploitation of the discontent over the jilting of 'Ofa-ki-Vava'u yielded a group united by a common cause although apart from 'Ofa and her immediate family, there was little support from other members of the hou'eiki. It was thought that Tungī would follow Baker, and Baker had certainly claimed so to Willis in late December 1899.[50] However no record remained of Tungī's involvement. Similarly Baker claimed in his December 1899 'petition' the support "at the Eastern End [of] the Chief Kalaniuvalu, who in heathen times was the sacred high priest of Tonga ... and the Chief of the Western End has also joined us" Eight families from Kalaniuvalu's village of Mu'a contributed to the 1900 misinale, but not Kalaniuvalu himself. Of the two families from Hihifo, Tongatapu listed in the 1900 misinale, both were commoners.

As noted above, the King was concerned about Baker's misrepresentation to Willis of the support of the hou'eiki for his Church, but it was likely that the continuing support for 'Ofa-ki Vava'u's cause definitely coloured his views of Baker's followers. Taemanusa, 'Ofa's mother, and her stepfather, Tevita Ula Afuha'amango, who came from an untitled Vava'u hou'eiki family, remained as the only significant high-ranking members following the tragically early death of 'Ofa-ki-Vava'u in December 1901. Baker used the *fale kautaha* belonging to Taemanusa in Siaine, Kolofo'ou, adjacent to the prison where Ula had earlier been chief gaoler, as his place of worship.

By the time Baker's followers had ejected him from the Church which he had founded, another member of the hou'eiki had emerged as their adviser. Tevita Polutele Kaho (later Tu'ivakanō) and his family had supported the cause of 'Ofa-ki-Vava'u but showed no record of having joined Baker's Church. Polutele had acted as interpreter in the negotiations to bring Willis to Tonga, and fulfilled a similar role once Willis arrived in June 1902. His subsequent involvement and rising political career are detailed in Chapter Four.

Among the leading commoners in Baker's Nuku'alofa Church were Sulio Taufa and his wife Namoe, (Namoe's daughter Kilisitina later married Polutele) Samuela and Siale Havili, Filipe and Lesieli Vea, Sione and Meleane Ikahihifo, Viliami and 'Ana Ongosia, Sione and Siale Finaulahi, Pita Vi, Siosaia and 'Alilia Nauha'amea, Uiliami Kalaniuvalu, Siosaia and Lātū Tu'iono and Siosifa Falepapalangi. Several students of Baker's schools were also to emerge as leaders in the years following Willis' arrival. Although Willis' records of reception into the Anglican Church from 1902 to 1904 were not to survive, a significant proportion of those who followed Baker in Nuku'alofa later showed some involvement in at least the first two years after Willis' arrival.[51]

The two congregations outside of Nuku'alofa were probably very small, and that at Hihifo had disappeared by the time of Willis' arrival. Usaia and Lolohea Kauvaka, one of the two families listed in the 1900 misinale, later played key roles in the Anglican Church in both Ha'apai and Nuku'alofa.

Little is known about the eight families at Mu'a listed in the 1900 misinale. Some of these people were later to be received by Willis into the Anglican Church, but showed no other involvement. It is likely that they left along with Taemanusa and other related families in 1904.

Those who requested that Willis come to Tonga in late 1901 claimed to be three hundred strong. Apart from Baker's 'petitions' and the list of contributors to the 1900 misinale, as printed in his *Niusipepa*, no other membership records of Baker's Church survived. From available records of Willis, and given that some reception records were either lost or destroyed by Willis following the loss of membership in 1904, this number was probably correct. There is no doubt about the continuity of membership of Baker's Church and those who became Anglicans in 1902.

Just how long these congregations, and Baker's Church as a whole, would have survived without the alternative leadership provided by Willis from June 1902 is a matter for conjecture. That there were some defections both before and after December 1901 was clear, both from the correspondence between the petitioners and Willis, and analysis and comparison between the few surviving documents of Baker's Church and Willis's incomplete records.

Membership certainly dropped in Lifuka, but given the fact that Baker lived amongst these people, it was hardly surprising. Mo'unga-one and Lape were bound by close family links both within and between these two small islands, and it is likely that they may have lasted as separate bodies for a few years at least without outside assistance. Although the Tongatapu membership had lost their focus of unity with the death of 'Ofa-ki-Vava'u, they were probably the best equipped, in terms of leadership, numbers and material resources necessary to support and run their own organisation.

As far as being a nationwide Church without outside assistance, the odds were set against them. The distance between islands was a barrier to effective organisation, as Willis was later to discover, and the peculiar distribution of the four main congregations would have made for great difficulties. The Roman Catholic Church, with strong outside support, in their sixty years in Tonga, had worked little outside their original areas in

Tongatapu, and had only established small followings in Lifuka, Neiafu and the Nuias. By comparison, hopes for the long term survival of Baker's Church, without Baker, looked slim.

There were no independent religious movements in that period in Tonga operating totally under local leadership. Even the Siasi Tau'ataina, independent from the Australasian Wesleyan Conference for seventeen years in 1902, had retained a palangi, the Rev'd Jabez Watkin, as their president. It was not that Tongans were incapable of running such an organisation, but there was still a tendency to look to Europeans to provide the skills and legitimisation, real or imagined, needed for their operation. This notion had its origins in the period of European contact prior to the arrival of the Wesleyan missionaries, where the beachcombers and escaped convicts who found their way to Tonga had been valued for the palangi skills they brought, and had often lived with the chiefly families. This had intensified and been institutionalised in the period which followed the arrival of the missionaries, and Europeans were seen by many Tongans as indispensable in such major leadership roles.[52]

Despite having been let down by Baker, a large proportion of former members of his Church were willing to obtain a European, sight unseen, to take his place.

# CHAPTER TWO - SOURCE NOTES

1 Jay 1983:10-11 2 The President condemned Pusey (Dr. M.G.A. Vale - Keeper of Archives to the writer: St John's College, Oxford 4/2/1988. 3 Wells Theological College- Record Book 1858-1859 (Wells Record Office WRO/2308/WTC/R/1a. See also Heeney 1976:6,96 A Different Kind of Gentleman. 4 Bird 1974: quoted in Restarick 1924:144 -unable to trace in 1906 ed. of Bird. 5 Muir 1951:328; Hopkins 1862 (2nd ed. 1866):417-418; Restarick 1924:201. The 1988 General Convention of the Episcopal Church declared a Feast of King Kamehameha IV and Queen Emma be observed on 28th September (Hawaiian Church Chronicle August 1988:3). 6 Teale 1983:203-204. 7 Restarick 1924:146, 149-150, 202. 8 ibid.:153, 160-161, 165, 168-172. 9 See discussion of the Cambridge Cambden Ecclesiological Society in White 1962:19, 34-35, 87. "Church Architectural Meetings" had been held at Wells Theological College during Willis' time as a student. Wells Theological College - Principal's Report for 1859 (WRO/2308/WTC/Prin.2). 10 Willis' Occasional Papers of the 1880s reported progress. He was disappointed that Queen Emma `overlooked' a bequest to the building fund in her will. (Willis 1886:3). 11 Restarick 1924:196-197. 12 Mark 1936:iv, 2-7; Kasten 1978:61. 13 Honolulu Bulletin of July 1891 quoted in Restarick 1924:192. Pacific Commercial Advertiser 19/5/1902; K. Perkins to writer: Honolulu 21/7/1988. 14 Restarick 1924:203. 15 Honolulu Diocesan Magazine quoted by Restarick 1924:174; Willis 1893:7-8. 16 Willis to Tucker: Honolulu 5/2/1896 (USPG/CLR/Honolulu 1871-1910/204-208). 17 Restarick 1924:176-177. 18 Willis 1896:10; Britsch 1986:135, 141ff; Restarick 1924:177; Lilioukalani 1898:269, 292. 19 Nevill to Archbp. of Canterbury: Shelton Rectory 7/2/1872 (Lambeth Palace Library vol.186 Canterbury Foreign 1871/182). 20 Pascoe Vol.1 1901:462-463; Licence of Alfred Willis issued by Bishop of London 7/4/1872 (JBP). 21 Restarick 1924: 148; Letters to Willis from Nevill: Dunedin 20/5/1885; Harper: Christchurch 29/1/1886; 26/4/1886; 15/7/1886; 9/10/1886 (JBP) 22.Willis to Tucker: Apia 18/4/1897; Pascoe Vol.1 1901: 463b. 23 Licence as in note 20 above, endorsed by Bishop Mandell 2/8/1897. 24 Willis to Tucker: Honolulu - letters in USPG/CLR/Honolulu 1871-1910/219-22, 222, 239; Lowe to Willis: St Albans 19/5/1899 (JBP); Montgomery to Willis: Hobart 7/3/1899 (NAF/DP/DT/3). 25 Willis 1899: 1-2 26.Floyd to Willis: Levuka 14/7/1899 (JBP); Whonsbon-Aston 1970: 48; F.T.19/8/1899, 23/8/1899. 27 Restarick 1924: 178-180. 28 Draft replies of Willis to Leefe (18/5/1900) and McLennan (n.d.) in JBP. 29 Copy in Willis' handwriting in JBP. 30 Tohi 1972: 46; Willis to Leefe: Honolulu (draft) 18/5/1900 (JBP). 31 George Tupou II to Willis: The Palace, Nuku'alofa 6/4/1900 (JBP). 32 Willis to George Tupou II: Honolulu n.d. (draft in reply to above); drafts to McLennan and Leefe as in note 28. 33 Copious correspondence between Willis and his cousin W.R.L. Lowe in JBP. 34 Restarick 1924: 180, 189; Honolulu Diocesan Magazine July 1900:260-266. 35 Pacific Commercial Advertiser 18/3/1902. 36 ibid.15/5/1902. 37 W. Beakbane to Willis: Honolulu 21/5/1902. 38 Tucker to Bp. of London: S.P.G., London 16/3/1900 (USPG/CLS/NZ&P/1842-1902/495); Tucker to Rev'd E.J. van Deerlin: S.P.G., London 27/6/1900 (USPG/CLS/NZ&P/2/1900- 1927/6). 39 Church Gazette of the Diocese of Auckland Oct 1900: 197; Willis to Archbp. of Canterbury: S.S. Ventura 2/6/1902 (Lambeth Palace Library/Davidson Papers/430/95- 97); Willis to Bp.Cowie: same date - as reprinted in New Zealand Guardian (Diocese of Dunedin) 1/10/1902: 10. 40 Niusipepa July 1900 - Misinale

Report. 41 Petition to Willis: Fakapale, Lifuka 23/10/1899 (JBP). 42 Niusipepa July 1900. 43 e.g. "Siasi Uesiliana 'o Toga - Koe gahi babitaiso na'e fai 'i he vahe ko Ha'afulihao" *Wesleyan Mission - Baptism Register for Vava'u* (Free Wesleyan Church Office, Vava'u) -no baptisms after 1887 for families who joined Baker's Church or later became Anglicans. For background see Rutherford 1971:126-138, 146-150; Forman 1978: 5; Lātūkefu 1974: 75; Ellem 1981: 160. 44 Notes taken by writer at a faikava: Hihifo, Lifuka 20/7/1988. 45 Minute Books of the Annual Conferences of the Free Church 1885-1905 (on Pacific Manuscripts Bureau Microfilm 979) 1899 & 1902; Niusipepa July 1900 -Misinale Report; 46 Anglican Church Register, Nuku'alofa (hereafter ACR):various refs. 47 ibid.; Niusipepa July 1900 - Misinale Report. 48 "Koe tohi fakamaoboobo 'oe gahi mali kuo fai 'i he Jiasi Uesiliana Tau'ataina 'o Toga 'i Vava'u" *Free Church - Marriage Register, Vava'u* (Free Wesleyan Church Office, Vava'u) ; interview with Kapatoka: Pukotala 25/7/1988; Niusipepa July 1900-Misinale Report (Mo'unga-one $112 Lape $102). 49 interviews with Kepueli Komiti: Mo'unga-one 28/7/1988; Lemani Taufa & others: Lape 5/4/1988; Finau Fatai: St Andrew's School, Longolongo 18/3/1988; Ko e Konisitutone (1904 ed.): 3 quoted in Tohi 1972: 67. 50 Baker to Willis: Lifuka 28/12/1899. 51 Niusipepa July 1900 - Misinale Report; ACR: various. 52 Lātūkefu 1974:34-35, 159-161; Cummins 1981:299 (especially for discussion of role of Dr. J.E. Moulton and his ha'a unga at Tupou College)

Shirley Waldemar Baker
NATIONAL ARCHIVES OF FIJI, SUVA

'Ofa-ki-Vava'u
NATIONAL ARCHIVES OF FIJI, SUVA

Shirley Baker and his daughter Beatrice, with Evi and Bernhard Becker
EDUARD BECKER COLLECTION, USED WITH PERMISSION OF DR. KURT DURING

Alfred Willis in his early years      Alfred Willis in his study
as Bishop of Honolulu          in Tonga 1902 or 1903
R. LOWE, LOWER HUTT         C.G. CAMPBELL COLLECTION

Alfred Willis with his layreaders, sometime prior to mid 1906
(Yim Sang Mark second from left)
NATIONAL ARCHIVES OF FIJI, SUVA

"Tongan girls dancing the `Lakalakas' [sic] on Pangaimotu" (1902 or 1903)
C.G. CAMPBELL COLLECTION, NEW YORK

"Kaitunu on the island PANGAIMOTU, August 1902"
C.G. CAMPBELL COLLECTION, NEW YORK

The Bishop's House, Kolofo'ou, Tongatapu
NATIONAL ARCHIVES OF FIJI, SUVA

The threefold order of ministry in apostolic succession in 1912  (from left)
Yim Sang Mark (priest), Alfred Willis (bishop) and Filipe Vea (deacon)
BISHOP JABEZ BRYCE PAPERS, SUVA

The altar, reredos and other sanctuary fittings brought by Alfred Willis
to Tonga in 1902 from his chapel at Iolani College.
NATIONAL ARCHIVES OF FIJI, SUVA

The `temporary' church of St Paul in the late 1920s. Note piles of rocks
prepared for the building of the `permanent' church.
NATIONAL ARCHIVES OF FIJI, SUVA

Yim Sang Mark with the choirboys of St Andrew's School in the 1920s
NATIONAL ARCHIVES OF FIJI, SUVA

Yim Sang Mark with the European congregation at Nuku'alofa around 1927
NATIONAL ARCHIVES OF FIJI, SUVA

Yim Sang Mark with Anglican Church members Nuku'alofa 1920s
NATIONAL ARCHIVES OF FIJI, SUVA

First Synod of the Diocese of Polynesia held in Suva 1925.
Seated centre left Archbishop Averill (N.Z.), centre right Bishop Kempthorne
Y.S. Mark standing second from left, H. Favell standing far right
NATIONAL ARCHIVES OF FIJI, SUVA

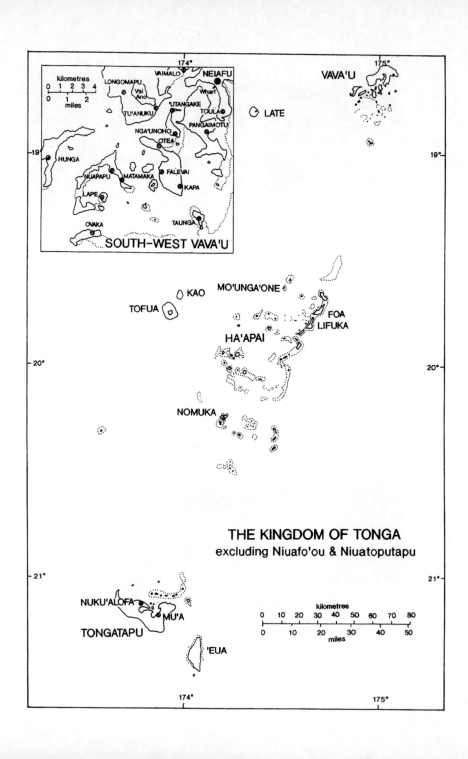

kilometres
0 1 2 3 4
0 1 2
miles

LONGOMAPU
VAIMALO
NEIAFU
VAI ANO
Wharf
'UTANGAKE
TOULA
TU'ANUKU
PANGAIMOTU
NGA'UNOHO
OTEA
HUNGA
NUAPAPU
MATAMAKA
FALEVAI
KAPA
LAPE
OVAKA
TAUNGA

**SOUTH–WEST VAVA'U**

174°
19°
19°
175°

VAVA'U

LATE

KAO
MO'UNGA'ONE
TOFUA
FOA
LIFUKA
**HA'APAI**

NOMUKA

20°
20°

**THE KINGDOM OF TONGA**
excluding Niuafo'ou & Niuatoputapu

21°
21°

NUKU'ALOFA
MU'A
**TONGATAPU**
'EUA

kilometres
0 10 20 30 40 50 60 70 80
0 10 20 30 40 50
miles

174°
175°

# CHAPTER 3

## ESTABLISHING THE CHURCH CATHOLIC...

. *"From island to island he has gone, carrying the Bible and Prayer Book, translating them into the native tongues, bearing the message of the Everlasting Gospel to the uttermost corners of the earth, his very presence an example and benediction." (Bishop S. Partridge giving tribute to Bishop Alfred Willis at the Lambeth Conference in 1920 USPG/CLR/NZ&P/ 1913-1927 /4/97 )*

### I

The Right Reverend Alfred Willis D.D., and Mrs Emma Willis arrived in Nuku'alofa on the mail steamer *Manapouri*, on Saturday 21st June 1902. They immediately set up home at Kolofo'ou in a house rented on their behalf by the petitioners.[1] By the second Sunday i.e. 29th June Willis had transformed the interior of the fale kautaha in Siaine into something resembling an Anglican church building. He dressed a newly constructed altar with the coverings, candlesticks and cross he had brought with him from his chapel at Iolani College, setting this with his chair and lectern on a raised platform. Behind this he placed a reredos depicting the crucifixion. This contrasted with the scene he had found the previous Sunday, of which he wrote, "There was a large table at which the officiant stood. Except for his surplice, there were no outward signs of the Church of England." *(Willis 1903:2)*

Willis was now ready to set about organising the Anglican Church in Tonga along strictly Catholic lines, being aware that "the teaching that the Tongans have received has left them in entire ignorance of the threefold ministry, of Confirmation, of Sacramental Grace and the Divine Law of Marriage." *("The Church in the South Seas" in Church Times 19/2/1904:248)* This meant to Willis more than introducing these missing elements and grafting them on to the lotu Uesiliana of Baker's former followers. His intention was to prevent the "many features of Wesleyanism in its Pacific development becoming stamped on the infant Church before its members could be instructed in a better way." *(Willis 1903:3)* Willis' first move was to receive the former followers of Baker into the Anglican Church, although, unlike his reception of Queen Lilioukalani in Honolulu, he did not administer hypothetical baptism or insist on re-baptism. The first group of fifteen men, being representatives of all of Baker's former congregations except Mo'unga-one, were received "into the Catholic Church" on Sunday 29th June. They included Tevita Ula Afuha'amango, Filipe Vea, Siosifa Falepapalangi, Samuela Havili, Siosaia Tu'iono, Pita Vi and Viliami Ongosia of Kolofo'ou; Saimone Fisilau of Mu'a; Talaiasi Tuli, Taniela Lutui and Simeona Vea of Lifuka; Sione Taufa and Metuisela Hoko of Foa; Usaia Kauvaka (shown as Mo'unga-one but from Hihifo, Tongatapu); and Melieli Kite and Lisiate Vehikite of Lape.[2] Those from the northern islands had travelled down to Nuku'alofa on the *Manapouri* when they heard that the Willises were on board. Willis confirmed the first four of these men on Sunday 6th July so as to be able to licence his first layreaders; Filipe Vea and Tevita Ula Afuha'amango for Tongatapu, and Talaiasi Tuli and Usaia Kauvaka for Ha'apai. The Ha'apai people returned to their islands on the *Manapouri* that evening.[3]

Willis travelled north to Ha'apai in late August, receiving people into the Church in Mo'unga-one, Lifuka and Lotofoa in early September. He confirmed many of these on another trip in April 1903.[4] He travelled to Vava'u in late October, where he both received and confirmed the people on Lape on 2nd November, 1902. He had already received and confirmed Siliveinusi Lavulavu in late July in Nuku'alofa before licensing him as a layreader.[5] On his return from Vava'u, Willis held a second confirmation service in the fale kautaha at Siaine on 30th November. This group, which consisted largely of women, included Taemanusa, Lesieli Vea, Sulio, Namoe and Kilisitina Taufa, Sione and Meleane Ikahihifo, 'Alilia Nauha'amea, Siosaia and Latu Tu'iono, 'Alilia Aho, 'Ana Ongosia and Siosifa Falepapalangi. These people received their first communion on Christmas Day 1902.[6]

Willis quickly turned his attention to what he considered a very high priority; the `correction' of the service of Baker's Church, which he found to be "incomplete and requiring careful revision." *(ibid.)* He had received a Tongan Bible, dictionary and Tongan grammar along with all the literature of Baker's Church from the petitioners before he left Honolulu. He soon considered that he had made sufficient progress in the Tongan language himself, having been deprived of Polutele Kaho's services as an interpreter soon after his arrival. Yim Sang Mark, then a boy of seventeen years of age, had arrived from Honolulu to join the Willises in August 1902, and he assisted with this work. It is unlikely that the competency of Willis and Sang

Mark was such that they worked without advisers in this early period. 'Ana Langi, who had joined the Bishop's household as Mrs Willis' maid soon after Sang Mark's arrival, was credited with checking the revised texts by Sang Mark in later years.[7]

Willis made few major changes to the services he had received from Baker, although those he made were important to him. He consistently replaced *Sihova* (Jehovah) with *'Eiki* (considering Lord a much more appropriate term than Jehovah) and purged Baker's Holy Communion service of the lotu Uesiliana term of setuata. Whilst some of his changes were purely the result of his desire to set the Anglican Church apart from lotu Uesiliana, others reflected his higher view of the sacraments and ministry. The use of *taula'eiki,* a pre-Christian term for priest, reflected a return to an Old Testament concept of mediator which equated with a more Catholic view of the priesthood. Willis reserved the commonly used faifekau for his layreaders.[8]

Similarly, Willis was concerned about the teaching expressed in the Nicene Creed, and with shades of fourth century controversy, corrected Baker's use of a Tongan term Willis considered to mean *homoiousios* - like substance, rather than *homoousios* - one substance. To Willis, this was yet another example of the inadequacy of the Nonconformists in expressing the true faith of the Church.[9]

Beginning with a revision of the Catechism in 1902, Willis consistently revised all the services produced by Baker which included Orders for Morning and Evening Prayer, Holy Communion, Confirmation and Baptism. Willis added the occasional services of the Burial of the Dead, Marriage, the Churching of Women and Private Baptism of Infants. In no way did he attempt to produce a Tongan liturgy. Like most of his Anglican contemporaries, he saw the *Book of Common Prayer* as the yardstick for the Church, and his aim was to produce what he considered to be the most accurate translation possible. Willis was dissatisfied with both translations of the Bible then in use in Tonga, and in the preparation of his Psalter and Lectionary, collated the two translations to produce what he considered to be the best possible form for use in worship. On Dr. Moulton's translation he commented "He has not kept strictly to the rules by which a translator should be governed and ... I could never sanction the use of his translation in public worship" *(Willis 1909:3)* Moulton's mistake was that he had used the then unpublished documents of the Revised Version in English, and not the Textus Receptus which, in 1880, was the recognised basis for all Bible

Society translations. In addition to this academic problem for Willis, the Moulton translation was only used by the followers of Wesleyan Mission and not the majority Siasi Tau'ataina, for reasons that had more to do with Tongan Church politics than accuracy of translation. Willis later attempted to produce a `corrected' translation of the whole Bible by this collation method, on which he was still working when he died. This was never published, the West translation of 1884, remaining the accepted version for Tongan Anglicans.[10]

Whilst the services of Baker had required merely revision, it was in the area of Church music that Willis made the most drastic outward changes. He was delighted by the new chants that Baker's daughters had taught for the canticles, but not so enamoured with "the hymnody of the Free Church at present in use by our people... [It is] altogether out of agreement with the Church's worship." *(Willis to Bishop of Dunedin: Nuku'alofa 31/3/1903 LPL/DP/430/117)* By 1905 he had translated over 100 hymns from *Hymns Ancient and Modern* , selecting what he considered suitable for the Catholic expression of the Faith. Over seventy of those selected were the products of hymn writers influenced by the Tractarian movement.[11]

Willis, in response to a request from the petitioners, had brought new anthems with him to Tonga, and he continued to supply his Church with what he considered to be suitable music for worship. The Tongan love of music suited Willis' particular view of what was `proper' in liturgy. A full choral service with use of vestments and two candles soon became normative Anglican worship in Tonga. R.T. Mathews, the Vicar of Suva visited Nuku'alofa in 1910 and later reported to the S.P.G.; "Bishop Willis was priest and Yim Sang Mark deacon. Full vestments were worn and the service was excellently sung" *(USPG/MR/1910/50)* E.H. Strong wrote in 1921that "the use here has been lights and vestments" *(Strong to Sec. of S.P.G.: Nuku'alofa 24/7/1921 USPG/CLR/NZ&P/1/110)* In true High Church style, Willis established a pattern of weekly Eucharist or Ante-Communion in Kolofo'ou, and considered that the only proper place for Holy Communion was following Morning Prayer.[12]

To guide the infant Church in what Willis considered to be the correct Anglican way, he desired two or three English priests to work with him. In his letters and publications of the first ten years in Tonga, this was a recurring theme.[13] This further reflected his Anglo-centric view which he attempted, with a large degree of success, to impose on the Anglican Church in Hawai'i,[14] and coloured his efforts to establish the threefold ministry in apostolic succession in Tonga.

Shortage of money, however, forced Willis to look to other avenues to fulfil his need for staff, and he soon began to make enquiries for the further training of Sang Mark. Willis' young assistant had been educated at Iolani College and had in addition received private lessons from Willis in Latin and Greek.[15] Although Sang Mark spoke good English , in addition to Hawai'ian and now Tongan, Willis desired that he be educated where he could improve his skills in Hakka, a North Chinese dialect. To this end, Willis applied in the first instance in late 1903 to a theological college in Shanghai, and later Hong Kong. These enquiries bore no fruit. [16]

Sang Mark eventually received a scholarship from Bishop Nichols of California to study at his college at San Mateo, which he entered in September 1906. He was ordained deacon by Nichols on 2nd June 1909. Sang Mark returned to Tonga in early September, having spent some time with his family in Honolulu.[17]

It was Alfred Willis' original intention that Sang Mark be ordained priest in Nuku'alofa, so that the people of the Church, whose only experience of ordained Anglican ministry was that of an elderly bishop, could have the opportunity to witness this very important occasion. However it was not to be, as William Floyd, the Vicar of Levuka and Willis' long time supporter, who had agreed to assist with the laying on of hands, died in late 1909. Frustrated in his efforts to find a substitute willing to travel to Tonga, the Bishop and Mrs Willis made a rushed trip to Auckland in late February 1910, and arranged that Sang Mark be ordained priest by Bishop Neligan in May that year.[18]

Sang Mark's entry into New Zealand was complicated by his Chinese origins, despite having been granted Tongan citizenship in 1904. The Dominion was at the height of its hysteria regarding Asiatic immigration, and protracted negotiations were required between Neligan and the Secretary of Customs, at one stage involving the Prime Minister, Sir Joseph Ward. This was not the first, or unfortunately the last, instance of Sang Mark suffering at the hands of Australasian Sinophobia. He had required the assistance of Thomas Trood in his capacity as Acting British Vice Consul in Apia, to enable his passage on a New Zealand-flagged ship to California in 1906.[19]

Despite all arrangements having been completed in New Zealand, Sang Mark was refused passage at Nuku'alofa until Willis signed an indemnity for any costs that may result from refusal of entry into Auckland.[20] In the event,

Sang Mark's ordination on Trinity Sunday at St. Mary's Cathedral, Parnell went without a hitch. He was ordained on Letters Dimissory from the Bishop in Polynesia, Tonga by this time being part of the newly-formed Diocese of Polynesia. But there was no doubt under whose authority he was to work in Tonga. In the declaration signed on the day of his ordination, Sang Mark pledged true and canonical obedience in all things lawful and honest to Bishop Willis in Tonga.[21] Alfred Willis now had an assistant priest for the work in Tonga whose concepts of the Church were probably nearer to his own than anyone whom Willis could import from England.

Willis' completion of the threefold order of ministry was similarly forced upon him by circumstances rather than design. He had long desired to visit England again, and when the opportunity came in 1912 for him and Mrs Willis to travel, Willis ordained Filipe Vea, his long serving layreader in Nuku'alofa as a deacon on 3rd March of that year.[22] Although he stated that this laid the foundations for a native ministry, this had never been the issue for Willis in the same way as the procurement of English priests to guide the Church on the proper path had been.

Indigenous ministry had never been of importance for him in Hawai'i either. In his thirty years in that country Willis had not ordained any native Hawai'ians, and his predecessor had ordained only one deacon, who later renounced his vocation and returned to politics.[23] This was despite one of the stated intentions of the establishment of the Hawai'ian Church being to relieve the Hawai'ians of their burden of cold Congregationalism. Of greater importance to Willis was correctness in theological outlook and Church practice, and a high standard of educational achievement, of a level which the Hawaiian population, native, European or Asiatic, was unlikely to attain. As a consequence, apart from two Chinese candidates, Willis had obtained all his staff from overseas, many directly from either his former parish of New Brompton or straight from English theological colleges. Willis had attempted to act in like fashion in Tonga.[24]

What training Willis gave Filipe Vea is unknown, but it appears likely that he had been forced to compromise on his normally high standards. He had requested information from the Church Missionary Society, who had a much stronger indigenous ministry in their missionary endeavours than the S.P.G., as to what training they gave their native ministry. Their reply, outlining the work in South China, where candidates were given sound Biblical study, Church history and doctrine, and the Prayer Book without English, Latin or Greek, would suggest that Willis followed this course.[25]

Whether Willis intended Filipe Vea to be ordained to the priesthood is unknown. Vea died in May 1913, only thirteen months after his ordination as a deacon. Given Willis' record in Hawai'i, where he waited four and eight years respectively before ordaining his Chinese deacons as priest, compared with an average of two and a half years for his English staff, it would seem unlikely. In addition, despite putting a new edition of his Tongan Prayer Book through the press *after* Filipe Vea was made a deacon, Willis did not include a service for the ordination of priests.[26]

Finance was always short in the mission of Alfred Willis, but this had not been a stated issue, in regards the ordination of Tongans, at the time of Filipe Vea's ordination. However Willis later considered it necessary "to wait and have a reasonable assurance that any who are ordained will be locally supported and will not look for a maintenance from foreign funds." *(Willis 1914:2)* After Filipe Vea's death in May 1913, Willis ordained no more Tongans. His silence on the whole issue of native ministry after that time would suggest that the short experiment had not been a success in his eyes, and he had no intention of ordaining any more Tongans.

Willis had relied on a form of local ministry since his arrival in Tonga. He had licensed his first four layreaders within two weeks of arriving in the Kingdom, and had extended this to all his congregations by 1903. These men were, in his eyes, on a level with the faifekau of the Siasi Tau'ataina and Fakaongo. They were licensed to conduct all services including the celebration of marriages,[27] with the exception of course of Baptism and Holy Communion. The layreaders were left on their own in their isolated churches for four to six months between the visits of Willis and Sang Mark. They were certainly recognised as the shepherds of their own flocks, both by their own people and those of other Churches. Willis attempted to direct their work from Nuku'alofa, sending sermon notes and other spiritual aids where possible. These untrained, unpaid ministers however worked somewhat independently, and remained for the bulk of Tongans, Anglican or otherwise, their main experience of Anglican ministry. In this they formed an unofficial fourth order.[28]

Consistent with his efforts to provide synodical government for the Church in Hawai'i, Willis gave his Tongan Church a constitution at their first council in May 1904.[29] This had no official standing outside Tonga, as the matter of jurisdiction had not at that stage been settled. Article I declared his Church in communion with the Anglican Church throughout the world, and Article II stated that Willis as bishop held ecclesiastical authority. He was reluctant to title the governing body a synod as his orders of ministry were incomplete. Instead, in Article IV he constituted a council, consisting himself as bishop, all licensed clergy, the layreaders plus one lay representative for each 'organised mission', with the power to add a lay interpreter or secretary if required.

Under Canon I of 'vested property', this council was also the board of trustees of the property and funds of the Church. Canon II concerned 'organised missions', Canon III of 'tithes and offering' permitting giving in kind as well as money, Canon IV of 'marriages' adopting the Table of Forbidden Decrees as in the *Book of Common Prayer* and prohibiting the remarriage of divorcees.

Discussion of the constitution and canons presumably took up the bulk of the 1904 council, although not all such meetings were restricted to such dry topics. The 1906 meeting discussed the problem of declining population in the Kingdom, Willis believing that the neglect of marriage was a major factor. It was resolved to send a petition to Parliament requesting some legislative inducement for men to marry at a younger age![30]

Further councils were held probably in 1909, either 1912 or 1914, and in 1918.[31] Mentions of the councils were infrequent in Willis' published reports, and the minutes, which were required to be kept in Tongan and English, were not known to have survived.

The constitution and canons were significant on two counts. Firstly, the powers of Willis as a bishop, which he believed were his by right of his consecration, were formally laid out and legitimised. Secondly, the constitution gave the Anglican Church in Tonga some badly needed public credibility, in a period when Willis considered the Church was still unrecognised by the Tongan Government.

Under Tongan law, land cannot be held as fee simple, and church buildings of all denominations are erected on land leased from the Government, or Royal or hou'eiki estate holders, subject to certain conditions being met. Government leases were preferred, as they were often granted free of rental, and so long as the land continued to be used for Church purposes, were normally renewed.[32]

The tenure of the fale kautaha in Siaine, which both Baker and Willis used as their place of worship in Kolofo'ou, had no legal standing, being used by permission of Taemanusa and her *kautaha ngatu*. Concerned about the insecure tenure, Willis had purchased the unexpired lease of a nearby acre from Dr. McLennan in 1903. Following a rumour that permission for the use of the fale kautaha would be withdrawn as soon as the Willises left for Fiji in June 1904, Willis and Sang Mark quickly drew up plans and ordered timber for a church to be erected on this property. This multi-purpose building was completed by Sang Mark and the Church members before the Bishop and Mrs Willis returned from Suva. Willis styled it the `temporary' Church of St. Paul. After the humiliation of the King by Sir Everard im Thurn in late 1904, the Government granted a quarter acre on a central site in Kolofo'ou. A schoolroom was built on this land in 1905, with a printing office and teacher's cottage added later.[33]

Protracted negotiations were held in 1910 with the Minister of Lands over the granting of what Willis believed to have been originally part of this same centrally located 'api, although occupied by the holder of an adjacent 'api. A lease was eventually granted for a little over an acre, on the condition that the Siaine property was surrendered. This exceeded all of Willis' expectations, and he was overjoyed that such a large site on the edge of the business section of the capital was available on which he could build a `permanent' church. In the meantime, he had to be content with the relocation of the wooden `temporary' church, which had been extended in 1906 with the addition of a schoolroom. Sang Mark, employing a new technique using a winch and coconut rollers he had learned whilst in California, set up this building on one corner of the 'api so as to leave room for future developments.[34]

Im Thurn's visit had also opened the way for the acquisition of the leases in Lape in 1905 and Mo'unga-one in 1907. In 1909 a site was granted in Ovaka, Vava'u, which had reverted to the Government as it was no longer occupied by the Wesleyan Mission.[35]

However in the more populous centres of Lifuka and Neiafu , the Government was not so forthcoming. Willis was required to purchase the lease of some land in Hihifo, Lifuka and a lease was not acquired in Neiafu until 1918. To Willis, it was important for the Anglican Church to have a physical presence in these steamer ports, despite the very small numbers of Church members, in order to counter the impressive edifices of the Roman Catholic missions. A small chapel with `prophet's chamber' attached was built on the Hihifo land in 1909, but it was to be left to his successors to erect a building on the Neiafu 'api and to build a `permanent' church in Kolofo'ou, Nuku'alofa.[36]

Encouraged by the success of Iolani College in Honolulu, Willis went to Tonga with the intention of providing grammar school style education for his

Church and the wider community. The 1901 petitioners believed that such a school would be a success if English were to be taught. Although a small school had been commenced in 1903, Willis considered its proper establishment to date from the opening of the school building on the newly acquired Kolofo'ou 'api by Sir Everard im Thurn in July 1905. This was staffed initially by Mrs Hargreaves, who was employed locally by Willis. When Sang Mark went to California in 1906, Willis employed Samuel Broadfoot, an Australian, as his printer, layreader and also schoolteacher.[37]

The school was not successful in its early years. Firstly, the perennial problem of finance was evident in the school, as in other areas of Church life. This was exacerbated by what Willis considered to be the Tongan unfamiliarity with the regular payment of school fees. Secondly, although when it opened, Willis' school was probably the only one in the Nuku'alofa area teaching English at a primary level, the Siasi Tau'ataina opened schools teaching English at this level in early 1907. These schools did not charge fees and several non-Church families withdrew their children, making the financial problems even worse.[38]

By 1910 Willis' day school was struggling to survive, and the students were confined to those from some Church families, with few younger children coming on to take the places of those who would be shortly leaving. The report of the Director of Education for 1913 made no mention of an Anglican school for that year, suggesting that by 1913 this school had folded.[39]

Willis had long stressed the desirability of establishing a boarding school. By doing so he believed that he could cater better for the children of Church families, particularly as they were more numerous in the outer islands than on Tongatapu. He had also long been concerned about the indolence of Tongan youth, and had written articles in his publications and in letters to friends overseas about the problem of juvenile smoking and other aspects of teenage behaviour.[40] Like the Wesleyan missionaries before him, who had been concerned about those who spent their time voyaging from group to group, Willis believed that he could correct, what he saw as "the utter want of discipline amongst Tongan youth" *(Tonga Church Chronicle No2 July 1913:3)*

When in England in 1912, Willis met up again with the Rev'd William Horsfall who was willing to return to Tonga to establish a boarding school, and also supply Willis' perceived need for an English priest. Willis was, as usual, frustrated by lack of money, the S.P.G. being unwilling to finance this development.[41]

St. Andrew's School was established in mid 1914 under the charge of Sang Mark, who in addition to teaching academic subjects, ran the school workshop and organised the school food gardens, whilst still acting as Willis' interpreter, secretary and assistant priest. The boarding school was not an immediate success, due to the financial problems caused by wartime shortages, and a succession of hurricanes since 1912. However the school developed a reputation for the competent teaching of English, and catered for many students outside the small Anglican community. The roll reached fifty five by 1919, twelve of these being boarders.[42] Several boys went on to St. Stephen's School in Auckland from St. Andrew's for further study. As had Iolani College in Honolulu, St. Andrew's School provided a base congregation for regular weekday services at St. Paul's Church, and the majority of those confirmed in Willis' final six years in Tonga were students of the school. Many of these did not continue active Anglican involvement once they left St. Andrew's, there usually being no active Anglican presence in their home areas. But the contribution made by Willis' school was considerable, as many ex-students went on to Tonga College and later secured employment with the Government or trading firms. This reputation was further developed in the 1920s by Sang Mark.[43]

Alfred Willis, like Shirley Baker before him, was well aware of the positive and negative power of the printed word. In Hawai'i he had generated a wide range of printed material, in the form of tracts and translation of polemical works, as well as the frequent defence of his position in the controversies which wreaked the Church. As a result, Willis had frequently generated sensational headlines in the local press. The availability of local printing facilities had been a concern to Willis before he moved to Tonga in 1902, and, as Baker had done before him, Willis initially sent his printing requirements to Wilson and Horton Limited in Auckland, the only press in Tonga being that belonging to the Government.[44]

Sang Mark, having learned printing skills at Iolani, set up a small press at the Bishop's house in 1905. Samuel Broadfoot operated the slow and ageing machine during Sang Mark's absence in California, moving the printing establishment to the Church 'api in 1908. Broadfoot completed the task of producing the Tongan psalter, collects, epistles and gospels before leaving Tonga in 1909.[45]

Seeing the printing establishment as a high priority, Willis tried in vain for several years to obtain a new machine. But it was not until Sang Mark and his wife 'Ana visited Honolulu in 1915, where he canvassed his old school mates and the congregation of St. Peter's Chinese Church for funds, that this need was filled. By this stage the major printing requirements of Willis's Church had been satisfied, a revised edition of the Tongan Prayer Book with Hymns having been printed in England in 1912. The capacity of the bigger machine was largely wasted.[46]

In addition to the production of regular services of the Church of England, Willis produced or translated as he had in Hawai'i, a wide range of tracts on aspects of the Church's life, catechisms and polemical works. They were printed in both English and Tongan defending the Church Catholic from her enemies within and without. These publications reflected Willis' wide range of interests and were written from his mid-Victorian High Church viewpoint, rejecting any notion of the scientific study of the Bible. Often they were produced in large quantities, indicating that their intended distribution was beyond the small Anglican community. Willis also produced a quarterly newspaper, the *Tonga Church Chronicle - Ko e Niusipepa ke fakamatala 'ae gaue 'ae Jiaji Faka-Igilani 'i Toga* between April 1913 and January 1915 which provided in addition to Church news and notices, a number of articles from a definitely anti-scientific standpoint.[47]

Throughout his Honolulu episcopate, Alfred Willis had relied heavily on the support of the Hawai'ian Mission Association, which had originally sponsored the establishment of the Reformed Catholic Church of Hawai'i Increasingly this organisation became dominated by the Willises' family and friends, including the Rev'd Phillip Willis (Alfred's younger brother), William Lowe (Willis' first cousin) and the Rev'd G.B. Simeon (Emma Willis' brother). They provided a significant proportion of Willis' financial support, in particular following the withdrawal of S.P.G. support in 1900.[48]

Willis had produced an annual report for this association and when he moved to Tonga he continued this practice. Laundered for his upper middle class readership, which now included a number from Hawai'i in addition to the English association, the *Annual Reports* contained little detail of the trials of the Mission and reflected a very Anglo-centric view of Tongan Anglican life. Apart from a listing of layreaders on the title page, he rarely mentioned any of the Tongan members by name. Willis studiously avoided contentious issues in the life of the Church, with only occasional allusions to internal or external problems.[49]

However as a means of raising of finance, the Tongan Mission Fund made a useful contribution, although never lived up to the initial expectations of Willis that it would provide three to four hundred pounds per annum. Alfred Willis received an annual private income of at least three hundred pounds and subsidised the shortfall of both overseas and local funds from this source, often going into debt to do so. [50]

From 1909, Willis received a grant from the S.P.G. of one hundred pounds, this annual grant being doubled from the beginning of 1913.[51] He considered this to be his personal stipend, and as with his private income, this sum never appeared in the published accounts of the Church. There was little consistency as to where Willis drew his funds from year to year for the ongoing expenses and for Sang Mark's stipend. His substantial personal contribution and absolute control of the finances failed to foster local initiative or responsibility. The funds raised in Tonga fluctuated wildly from year to year, and depended upon the price of copra and the fortunes of Europeans employed by the Tongan Government and local trading firms. Willis' original aim to make the Anglican Church in Tonga self-supporting failed, resulting in, by 1920, almost total dependency on outside funds for its existence.[52]

## II

Alfred Willis had inherited around three hundred Tongans from Baker's Church, in five distinct communities having little or no physical connection with each other. Baker had seen no use for work amongst the European population in his efforts to re-establish himself in Tonga. Willis was, on the other hand, able to justify and legitimise his presence in the Kingdom by the responsibility he saw to the Europeans living in Tonga, after what he considered to be years of criminal neglect by the Anglican Church of their spiritual needs.[53] The Bishop and Mrs Willis were resident in Kolofo'ou, and it was here that their presence was most strongly felt amongst both the Tongan and palangi communities.

Willis was able most successfully to make the changes he saw necessary to firmly establish the Church in this, the most urbanised of all Tongan communities. The ability of Baker's former followers to maintain their independence after the death of 'Ofa-ki-Vava'u indicated their distance from traditional rural power structures. Polutele Kaho, and Taemanusa and Tevita Ula Afuha'amango, the highest ranking members of the post-Baker Church, provided the leadership that was required in the six months before Willis arrived.

The mutually beneficial relationship between Polutele and Willis soon became obvious as the political events of the first decade of the century unfolded. Despite his close relationship with Sulio Taufa, Namoe and Kilisitina, Polutele did not lead a party within Willis' Church. This enabled him to act in an expedient manner within the Church as he did in politics. As such, he was not a threat to the authority of Willis.

Tae and Ula were in a different situation. As the mother and stepfather of 'Ofa-ki-Vava'u, they had made considerable sacrifices for her cause and Baker's Church. Ula, who had been chief gaoler, lost his job for using the prisoners to cut copra for the 1900 misinale of Baker's Church.[54] The death of their daughter had shifted the focus to themselves.

Willis initially secured Ula's support by licensing him as one of his layreaders, and a close relationship developed between the Bishop's household and this key family. Dr. Clarence Gordon Campbell, a wealthy American amateur anthropologist visited Tonga with his wife and daughter on two occasions in 1902 and 1903.[55] Dr. Campbell's extensive photographic collection and Helen Fahnestock Campbell's diaries give one of the few contemporary glimpses of Anglican Church life in Nuku'alofa in these early years. She wrote;

"Aug.27th [1902] - Bishop and Mrs Willis "musical evening". About fifteen men and women of the Tongan choir English Church sang for us. Many intricate selections wonderfully rendered. Excellent tunes, Christmas anthems, an "Ode to Ofa" and many sacred selections. ....Polutele, Tae, the high chiefess, and Ula were among the party...

Aug.31st - Early communion in morning at 7.30 in Pro Cathedral (Tae's Tapa House). At the McLennans to luncheon. After lunch Tae came and said she wanted to adopt the child. She called her Ofa, Tehina Aki Ofa, child chiefess Ofa (a very great compliment), the first time she has given the name to any foreigner...

Aug.9th [1903] - Went to 10.30 service at the English Church (held in Tae's tapa house). Officers and blue jackets for the "Sparrow" there ....Went at 3 o'clock to the Tongan service in the English church. Ula (Tae's husband) preached. Very pretty music. Cocoa later at Mrs Willis'. Polutele came in the evening..."

But all was not well with Willis' relationship with this key family, who led a major party within the Kolofo'ou congregation, and through Tae's family connections, probably had influence in the small group of Baker's former followers in Mu'a. Willis had learned a little from his Honolulu experience and declined to display his dirty linen in public in his efforts to make the changes he considered necessary to bring this group of dissenting Tau'ataina into the Anglican fold. In addition, since the death of 'Ofa-ki-Vava'u and the demise of Baker, the fortunes of the small Anglican community had ceased to be of interest to the newspaper-reading public of Fiji and Tonga. As a consequence, few details survived of what, by early 1904, became a major dispute within the Kolofo'ou congregation. This led to the defection of Tae and Ula, a group of their followers, and probably the whole Mu'a congregation.

It is likely that problems arose from a combination of factors. Firstly, unlike Baker, Willis was determined to make considerable changes in forms of worship, structure and doctrine in line with his views of the Church true and Catholic. As in Hawai'i, this was possibly seen as imposing foreign ideas that had little relevance to local people. That the bulk of Tongans did not become Anglicans upon observing what Willis believed to be such a superior form of Christianity, would reinforce this.

Secondly, Willis was intent on being not only the sole source of *'ulunganga faka-Siasi Ingilani,* but as in Hawai'i, to be also the temporal head of his Church. Having accepted Baker's authority more or less without question, with disastrous consequences, Tae and Ula were possibly unwilling to risk a second fiasco.

Thirdly, the members of the Anglican Church were still somewhat treated with indifference by the Government due to Polutele's political ambitions and Willis' close relationship with the British Agent and Consul and other agents of perceived threats to Tonga's independence. It is possible that Ula saw that his interrupted government career and family fortunes would be better served by leaving Willis' Anglican Church. Ula was in fact re-appointed to his old job as chief gaoler in 1905. His daughter, 'Ana Seini Takipo, and therefore a half-sister of 'Ofa-ki-Vava'u, married the widowed King in 1909. The following year, the King desired to create a noble title and tofi'a for Ula, but was prevented from doing so by the Parliament.[56]

Willis was naturally disappointed at the drop in membership that resulted from this dispute with Tae and Ula. But it did enable him to consolidate his power in his infant Church amongst those who remained, as both their spiritual and temporal head. The Kolofo'ou congregation consisted of some very strong and independent people, many of whom were older and widowed, whose children were frequently were not members of the Church, and a number of younger individuals whose families were not Anglicans.

These people had already made the break from traditional structures, and had little to lose by any further changes that Willis would make.[57]

Secondly, those family links which did exist were important, and came into sharper focus once Tae and Ula left the Church. The daughters of Viliami Langi, a Tau'ataina minister, and his wife Selai, were probably of most significance. Filipe Vea, Willis' other layreader and later deacon, was married to Lesieli, the eldest Langi daughter. Sang Mark's involvement with the Langi family, particularly following his marriage to 'Ana in February 1911, further enabled a direct link from Willis into this key family. Sang Mark's easy manner and skills in the Tongan language promoted Willis' view among a wide group of the Tongan membership of the Church.[58]

In addition, Alfred Willis, despite his reputation for peevishness in matters ecclesiastical, had a strong pastoral ministry, frequently visiting both Church members and the families of the school children who were not Anglicans. Just as with the work he had initiated amongst the Chinese and Japanese immigrants in Hawai'i' Willis saw a responsibility to the Niueans who had been brought to Tonga to work as labourers for the Public Works Department. They had not integrated well into Tongan society, and tended, with some notable exceptions, to live together at Halafo'ou. The Niueans were of an London Missionary Society background, but despite the work of Willis and Sang Mark in this community, only a small number of Niueans became Anglicans.[59]

After the initial receptions by Willis into the Church in 1902, few new members joined the Kolofo'ou congregation until the establishment of St. Andrew's School in 1914. With the exit of Tae and Ula, the deaths of some older key members in the early years, and the small numbers of young people in the congregation, Anglican membership declined to between fifty to sixty in number by 1910, and stayed at about that level for the remainder of Willis' ministry.[60] As numbers dwindled, so did the lay leadership in Kolofo'ou, and those who remained were becoming older and therefore less able to give as much energy to the Church as in earlier years. After Filipe Vea's death, Willis moved Talaiasi Tuli down from Ha'apai to work with the Kolofo'ou congregation. Tuli returned home in 1915 and no new layreader was appointed.[61]

As with the other congregations, the influenza epidemic or *mahaki faka'auha* of 1918 took its toll in Kolofo'ou, claiming victims of all ages, including potential leadership of the Church. Tevita Vea, a son of Lesieli and the late Filipe, who was a teacher at St. Andrew's School, and Tevita

Vailapa, a son of Usaia Kauvaka, both died in the epidemic, in addition to a number of key older members.[62] The picture presented of the Kolofo'ou congregation in 1920 was one of a group of older people, a mere handful of potential young leaders, and a number of schoolboys from non-Church families, with generally weak leadership. All this did not augur well for the future of Willis' Anglican Church.

The European community of Nuku'alofa of the late nineteenth and early twentieth century has often been described as a `beach' community due to its growth near a trading port. As such, it had much in common with Levuka, Apia and Honolulu in an earlier period. But due to the prohibition on the purchase of land by foreigners in the Kingdom, the resulting community was both poorer financially and less populous than these other `beach' settlements in the Pacific. As a result, Nuku'alofa largely avoided the excesses of public drunkenness and vagrancy which was often a feature of such communities.

By 1902 the European community consisted of a number of traders of predominantly German and British origin, most of whom had spent many years in the Pacific. Many had married Tongans or Samoans. In addition, there were a small number of expatriates who worked for the Tongan Government, whose stay in the Kingdom was normally of short duration. A handful of Australian Wesleyan missionaries, French Catholic priests and the Rev'd Jabez Watkin and his family, who were the only palangi who had a significant role in the Siasi Tau'ataina, made up the balance of the European residents.

The British Government was represented by the newly appointed Agent and Consul, Hamilton Hunter, and the German Government by the Vice Consul, Waldemar von Treskow, a planter and retired trader who had lived in Tonga for over twenty five years. The British representative and the Wesleyan missionaries lived in Kolomotu'a, and the Roman Catholic bishop and priests had their base at Ma'ufanga. The balance of the European residents, who numbered around two hundred in 1902, lived as the Willises' neighbours in Kolofo'ou.[63] As a bishop in the Church of England, Willis had certain social responsibilities and obligations, and whatever the King and Government may have felt about his coming to Tonga, the European community, on a social level at least, accepted his presence. No social occasion in this small and introverted community was complete without their attendance, which was frequently noted in contemporary newspaper reports.[64]

The religious background of this community was varied, even among those few who attended Willis' services. Those Germans of Lutheran background, with a higher view of the sacraments than other Protestants, could more easily accommodate themselves to Willis' view of the Church.[65] But the same could not be said of the bulk of the European residents, whom Willis believed had abandoned their religious obligations. Bishop Twitchell of Polynesia considered however that Willis, "whilst active, is too old for the work and has lost the `attractive power' so necessary in a colony of beachcombers" *(Twitchell to Montgomery: Suva 22/2/1909 USPG/OLR/1910-1911/196/58)* Willis' heavy penitential emphasis, with the frequent use of the Litany, long services (never less than Mattins, Ante-communion and Sermon) and lengthy and heavily intellectual addresses had little appeal. This community had existed for many years quite happily without the benefits of the Church true and Catholic, and saw little need now.[66]

Willis struggled on with a few Europeans and part- Europeans of longer residence, but the bulk of his congregation were drawn from amongst the diplomatic community and government employees. Their tenure in the Kingdom was generally of short duration, and in the political upheavals that punctuated Willis' first ten years, often terminated at short notice. European Church life, in common with the accepted mores of Nuku'alofa society, was led totally separate from the Tongan majority. Numbers remained small, a fact which Willis was soon resigned to.[67] This reinforced his resolve that his mission was to establish the Church amongst the Tongan people where he felt he was more appreciated, and he could, at least in his terms, see more consistent progress. It was in that area he put his real energies.

But Mrs Emma Willis lacked enthusiasm for the work in the Kingdom, either amongst the European or Tongan communities. She found the climate, after Honolulu, both physically and social fatiguing, and was frequently absent in New Zealand. She spent most of 1906 and the early part of 1907 in England where she hoped her husband would be able to join her. She was reconciled however, to the fact that he was committed to the work in Tonga, and had little desire to reside permanently in England again.[68]

Emma Willis was twenty years younger than the Bishop, and in addition to moving to the social obscurity of Nuku'alofa, had taken a substantial drop in income and standard of living. Willis, although disappointed that she was unable to share fully in his vision, was somewhat understanding of her situation. He wrote to Bishop Montgomery at the S.P.G. in early 1912; "My wife has to do without many things I wish she could have. It may not be generally known (though the fact is recognised by medical men) that the climate of Tonga is much harder on the female than the male sex due to the absence of hills. There is no getting at anytime above sea level, and to get a change of air at all a horse and carriage becomes a necessity and ceases to be a luxury. But this my wife has had to do without these ten years." *(op.cit. Nuku'alofa:15/2/1912 USPG/CLR/NZ&P/2/271)* In early 1916 Emma Willis suffered a complete physical and nervous collapse, and she travelled firstly to Auckland, and later to England to live with her brother Algernon Simeon. She never returned to Tonga.[69]

Mrs Willis did get a change of air on the few occasions that she accompanied the Bishop on his visits two or three times a year to the congregations in the northern islands. Here a different picture of Anglican Church life grew up from that in Kolofo'ou. Each isolated congregation had developed some unique features.

In Baker's former base of Hihifo, Lifuka, numbers remained very small during the entire period of Alfred Willis' work in Tonga. Describing the Mission in Lifuka in 1906 as `not yet organised' (i.e. under Canon 2 of his constitution), he felt that many would join if there was a church building, services having been held in the house of Talaiasi Tuli since the breakup of Baker's Church. However the long awaited `movement towards expansion' never occurred, despite the fact that a land lease was acquired and the Chapel of the Holy Trinity built in 1909.[70]

There were three major reasons for the poor response which Willis received in Lifuka. Firstly, those few people who remained with the Church after the split with Baker were mostly older, a feature in common with most of Willis' congregations. There were only eight baptisms in the period to 1912, and one past that date.

Secondly, following the death of Filipe Vea in 1913, Willis moved Talaiasi Tuli to Tongatapu, thus weakening the leadership of the already struggling congregation. Usaia Kauvaka, whom Willis sent to take Tuli's place, did not stay long. After Tuli's return to Lifuka in 1915, rejoined the Siasi Tau'ataina, where he became the choir leader, his talents in this area always having been in demand. Willis appointed two further layreaders, but sickness and death ended their work, and he could find no one to take their place.[71]

Thirdly, there were already much stronger groups providing religious options in Lifuka. The Seventh Day Adventists and the Roman Catholic mission, with the additional attraction of a school, were well established in Ha'ato'u. Those boys from Lifuka who studied at St. Andrew's School were usually confirmed in Nuku'alofa, but on returning to Lifuka and finding no strong Anglican congregation to nurture them, returned to the Siasi Tau'ataina or found a home in another denomination.[72]

Willis attempted to work amongst the Europeans in Lifuka, but this suffered from similar problems to that of the Kolofo'ou European congregation; small numbers, the generally short stay of those who were interested, and a general lack of interest on the part of the small trading community. In addition, many of the long term residents were married to Tongans, and if they had any interest in matters religious, they normally followed the denomination of their spouse.

The Tongan congregation at Lotofoa survived only as long as Sione Taufa was resident there as layreader. Willis did not regularly visit Foa. The communicants, who in 1906 only numbered three, travelled to Lifuka to take the sacraments. Willis had received a part-European family from Foa into the Church in 1907, along with additional members of the family of Sione Taufa. No further ministry was practised in Foa after that year, as Taufa moved to Mo'unga-one to take up the position of assistant layreader.[73]

The Church which developed in Mo'unga-one was in Willis' early years at least, very different from the other Ha'apai congregations. Isileli Talo, who Willis licensed as layreader in 1903 to replace Usaia Kauvaka, provided strong leadership for the first decade. Services were originally held in a frame building belonging to Siosaia Hausia. By November 1907, a European-style church dedicated to St. Philip and St. James had been built with funds largely provided by the local congregation. Willis consecrated this building in August 1908.[74]

Most of the people in the northern portion of Mo'unga-one's only village became Anglicans, and a strong Church life developed, encouraged by the frequent visits of their Anglican relations from Lape. Willis' visits to this isolated island were not only appreciated by the Anglican community. Few ministers, Tongan or European, visited this isolated island, and the whole population usually turned out to welcome the Bishop.[75]

However Mo'unga-one exhibited one feature that was common to both the other Ha'apai and Kolofo'ou congregations; the absence of younger people in the Church. There were a large number of widows, and only three baptisms after 1911. Only a small number of boys attended St. Andrew's

School, those returning finding the Church weak or non-existent.[76]

The final demise of the Church in Mo'unga-one came from a combination of factors beyond the control of Willis or his congregation. Mo'unga-one was a very difficult place to land a boat, there being a choice of an unprotected beach subject to the tides and the prevailing wind, or two rocky coves on the south and west of the island. The journey to Lifuka always required careful synchronisation and was frequently disrupted by rough seas. Shipping services provided by the Union Steam Ship Company of New Zealand Limited were initially cut by half at the outbreak of the First World War, and as the war proceeded, they were run on erratic schedules. The visits of Willis and Sang Mark to all their island congregations, including Mo'unga-one, were consequently infrequent.[77]

The loss of key leaders in the congregation, including the moving of Sione Taufa to Lifuka in 1915, and the death of Isileli Talo in 1917, weakened the Church at a crucial stage of its life. The mahaki faka'auha of late 1918 devastated the remaining membership of all ages, with the deaths of at least six adults from the congregation. Among those who died was Isileli Talo's son Saleteli Atu, whom Willis had appointed as layreader earlier that year when he had made his first visit in many months to the island.[78] This once vigorous congregation was reduced to a mere handful and their chances of future survival as Anglicans looked grim.

Alfred Willis took the most pride in his congregation in the southern islands of Vava'u. Under the leadership Siliveinusi Lavalavu for the entire period of Willis' Tongan ministry, they made up the largest group of Anglicans outside of Nuku'alofa. They were centred on the tiny island of Lape, of which Lavulavu was a matapule, and where Willis had received and confirmed the entire population as Anglicans in November 1902.

The Church quickly spread through existing family links and the movement of people from Lape, to the adjacent islands of Ovaka and Nuapapu. The people of Lape were the first of Willis' congregations to build a church, doing so in 1905 at their own expense, in Tongan style with an iron roof. This was styled St. Andrew's and consecrated by Willis in February 1906.[79] Unlike the rest of Willis' other congregations, there were people of all ages involved. After St. Andrew's School opened in 1914, several boys from Lape and Ovaka were educated there, some going on to further study at St. Stephen's School in Auckland.[80]

In the much larger village of Ovaka, the Anglicans remained a minority. They built the Church of St. Luke the Evangelist, in European style, on a prominent site in the centre of the village in 1916. As in Mo'unga-one, there was a good relationship with the local Tau'ataina, who often combined with the Anglicans to celebrate major events in Church life.[81]

Willis built up a warm and close relationship with these Vava'u people, who in appreciation of his efforts built a house for his accommodation during his visits to Lape, and a `prophet's chamber' as part of their house on their 'api kolo in Neiafu. Willis, in return, frequently helped his Vava'u congregations with the provision of food and supplies during the droughts and hurricanes which were a feature of the period.[82]

The key to Willis' success was the use of Lavulavu as his agent in establishing the Anglican Church in Lape and the adjacent islands. His exploitation of the best educated and most personally powerful of all his local layreaders was possibly initially unconscious, but Willis' innocence could not have lasted long in this regard. The alliance was mutually beneficial. Lavulavu, in common with all of Willis' layreaders, attained status on a level with that of the Tau'ataina faifekau, with the added advantages gained from a close relationship with, and frequent visits of, a palangi of the rank and bearing of Willis. These Vava'u congregations resembled most closely traditional Tongan structures which Willis so disliked in the lotu Uesiliana, and it was ironic that his greatest success story was largely due to these factors.

The same could not be said for the Anglican Church in Neiafu, which despite Willis' efforts to make it otherwise, remained little more than a transit point on his trips to Lape. His major involvement were the frequent baptisms from a small number of European and part-European families, including eight children of Willis' Honolulu acquaintance, Thomas Rudling. The first communion service was not held until 1909, with only three communicants attending.[83] From about 1911 to 1916, Miss Kathleen Howard taught at the European School in the northern capital, before returning to Tongatapu due to ill health, where she died in 1917. She attempted to encourage Anglican work, but with little result. [84] As with Lifuka, many of the long term resident traders were married to Tongan women, and followed the religious inclination of their wives. Neiafu never had an effective Anglican presence, Tongan or European, in Willis' lifetime.

### III

Alfred Willis' vision of the Church Catholic becoming the National

Church of Tonga, reuniting the disaffected branches of Wesleyanism under its umbrella, was even less likely by 1920 than it had been when he first mooted the idea in 1897 during the campaign to establish the Anglican Church in Samoa. Willis had failed to even keep the membership which he had inherited from Baker's Church in 1902. Willis' failure was a combination of his own attitudes and expectations, and circumstances, geographical, religio-cultural and political in nature, whose importance he had been unable or unwilling to grasp, and others which were beyond his control.

Willis was a product of the mid Victorian period and took with him to Tonga, as he earlier had to Honolulu, an elevated Anglo-centric view of the Church and the world. He failed, as he had in Hawai'i, to plant this deep in the rich spiritual and cultural soil of either of these island Kingdoms. In common with many missionaries, and the Wesleyans had been no exception in Tonga, he attempted to transplant *in toto* his denominational system. The Anglican Church had grown up in England over the centuries in response to a series of factors which were peculiarly English. Willis had the expectation that it would be rapidly adopted and assimilated in Tonga.

But Willis misjudged Tongan society, which outwardly showed signs of being Anglicised, but whose Euro-American acculturation has been compared with that of Japan.[85] Dr. Clarence Gordon Campbell had described the Tongans to the Archbishop of Canterbury in 1903 as "not a finer primitive people in the world... particularly well fitted to receive the full benefits of the teaching of our Church." *(op.cit. Cairo 21/3/1904 LPL/DP/430/161- 165)* But material and religious changes that had been adopted were by choice or expediency rather than having been forced from outside. Under this veneer, many traditional concepts still flourished, this being as true within lotu Uesiliana, as the major religious force in the Kingdom, as in other areas of Tongan life.

Willis came up against something that was much deeper than purely denominational practice. The alliance of Taufa'ahau (later King George Tupou I) and the Wesleyan missionaries from the 1830s had been mutually beneficial, enabling the consolidation of his power with a new religious base, (not withstanding his own deep Christian faith) and fulfilling the desire of the missionaries to spread their gospel. In spite of the efforts of the missionaries, and contrary to the outward appearance of Wesleyan worship and many church buildings, the Church which had resulted had taken over many of the pre-Christian functions of the old religious and social order. The more obvious of these functional substitutes could be found in the practices of Sabbath *tapu, talitali malanga, kai fakaafe,* the wearing of *ta'ovala,* and fakamisinale.[86] Willis had described this lotu Uesiliana to Bishop Nevill in 1902 as "probably the most degraded Christian religion in existence" *(Nevill to Abp. of Canterbury: Dunedin 6/7/1903 quoting letter from Willis LPL/DP/430/134-135)* He was determined not to allow its influence to pervade his Church. He therefore brought with him to Tonga the Anglican form to completely replace this, and was not content just to sow the seed, but to build a structure, however inappropriate, of which he oversaw every detail.

The model Willis introduced was one with a heavy sacramental emphasis, a high view of the priesthood and a parochial model designed for the English countryside. He built up an expectation amongst his congregation that they frequently receive the sacraments. He was unable to fulfil this, either with the English clergy he would have preferred, or by ordaining Tongans, whom he considered as yet lacking in the educational attainment necessary. In addition, Willis' visits to his island congregations had relied on a regular shipping service; when this was reduced and disrupted by the First World War, these problems were compounded. The mahaki faka'auha of 1918 reduced these already weak centres of Anglican work to a point where their future survival was uncertain.

Willis' Tongan Mission had many parallels with that of the Anglicans in Korea. Founded in 1890 on similar High Church notions to those of Alfred Willis, and totally dependent on overseas staff and funding, the leaders of that Church also believed that part of the mission to Korea was to reunite the various factions and sects in that country into the Church true and Catholic. They faced similar problems to those of Willis, with scattered congregations who had been taught the importance of the reception of the sacraments, which were subsequently unable to be fulfilled. The Korean Church struggled to survive. It was slow to develop a native ministry, the local Church members having received an understanding of the priesthood which set it so high, both in terms of theology and educational attainment, that it could be achieved by only an elect few. The Korean Anglican Church suffered near extinction when the English staff were forced to withdraw during the Japanese occupation.[87] A similar picture may have developed in the Hawai'ian Church if not for the large groups of Asiatic immigrants with whom Willis worked in that country.

The wholesale transplantation of the theology and ideals of the somewhat grandiose missionary bishopric movement to distant lands without modification from the mid nineteenth century onwards was not always successful. Tonga, as a late example of this approach, was a case in point.

The efforts to establish the Anglican Church in Tonga had some features in common with other second wave denominations whose missionaries entered the Kingdom in the same period. The Seventh Day Adventist and Latter Day Saints missionaries also worked amongst Tongans who had been originally converted to Christianity by the Wesleyan missionaries. They relied on overseas sources of finance, initially drew their staff from overseas, and attracted a portion of their converts through the provision of educational opportunities. They provided, like Willis' mission, potential religious and temporal alternatives to the established order, their doctrine, practice and authority structures differing greatly from the lotu Uesiliana.

Their approach differed from that of Willis, as they insisted on re-baptism of their converts. Willis believed that his mission was to consummate the inadequate, but not invalid form of Christianity that the Tongans had received. To Willis of course, the Seventh Day Adventists and Latter Day Saints were `sects' and totally invalid! Willis, in common with many Anglicans of his period, considered that proselytism was not the correct approach to increase the membership of the Church true and Catholic. He believed that the following of Baker by some hundreds of people was part of a spontaneous movement led by the Holy Spirit. Once properly established, the superiority of Willis' fuller Christianity would become obvious to the rest of the Tongan population.

His approach contrasted with the vigorous proselytism of the Adventists and L.D.S., who did not have the luxury of the ready made congregations such as Willis had inherited from Baker's Church. But the fortunes of both of these bodies in their early years somewhat resembled those of Willis' Church, for some of the same reasons.

Census figures for religious profession showed:

|  | 1911 Tongan | Others | 1921 Tongan | Others | 1931 Tongan | Others |
|---|---|---|---|---|---|---|
| Latter Day Saints | 87 | 15 | 453 | 41 | 667 | 61 |
| Seventh Day Adventist | 25 | 18 | 38 | 38 | 186 | 46 |
| Anglican | 185 | 153 | 133 | 127 | 175 | 136 |

*(Source - Tonga Government Gazettes)*

The Adventists relied almost totally on European missionaries until the early 1920s. They expected the instant adoption by their Tongan converts of both a more ascetic life-style and a very different religious system. Their efforts in education tended to be centralised rather than village-based. As a result, they had more success amongst urbanised Tongans, Europeans and part-Europeans. It was not until a consistent policy of indigenous ministry was adopted from the 1920s that membership began to grow.[88]

The L.D.S. missionaries began work in the Kingdom using American missionaries in 1891. They had gained only sixteen converts by the time they withdrew in 1897. They re-entered from Samoa in 1907 and recommenced their work in Vava'u, and by 1909 had three congregations in the Neiafu area. Their policy of establishing schools in rural villages, consolidation in a small area, and early adoption (somewhat forced on them by Government policy that restricted the entry of American missionaries) of an indigenous ministry, all resulted in a spectacular growth in numbers.[89] This was in a period when Anglican membership was static in Tongatapu and Vava'u, and falling in Ha'apai.

The sipinga of lotu Uesiliana had been accepted by the majority of the Tongan population, including the Royal household. Both the members of the Siasi Tau'ataina and Siasi Fakaongo saw themselves as standing in the tradition, both spiritual and temporal, of King George Tupou I and saw little reason to change from this. The reality was that Alfred Willis, the Adventists and the L.D.S. were all latecomers in the Kingdom. The more vigorous approach of these latter bodies, using Tongan missionaries and providing a more accessible education system, was more likely to succeed.

Alfred Willis had seen for himself a place in the hierarchy of Tongan society as an Anglican bishop. There certainly were parallels with the leadership of both the Rev'd Jabez Watkin and Dr. Moulton in their respective Churches, which could have been seen from outside as episcopal in nature.

E.W. Gifford, an American anthropologist, witnessed the scene in Lifuka in 1920 when Watkin was carried shoulder high, small boat and all, from the water to the dry land, by ten Tau'ataina ministers.[90] Willis had a similar experience when he arrived in Lape in 1916 to make preparation for the consecration of the new church building at Ovaka.[91] Willis' particular view of himself as a bishop of the Church true and Catholic had little relevance for anyone outside his small group of followers. In fact, his very identification with a Church that was overtly English in name and outlook, was for the first years of his residence in Tonga, to work against its progress.

Willis had pinned his hopes on establishing the Anglican Church in Tonga, with all the implications that he understood would follow, on Royal sponsorship of his mission. In this he hoped to repeat, and if possible, improve on the example of Hawai'i. Unfortunately for him, political circumstances changed very rapidly in the Kingdom, and if there had ever been any slight hope of Royal patronage in early 1900, this was certainly dashed by the events of May 1900 and following.

Willis miscalculated badly in that when he did come in 1902, without the King's sponsorship, or even prior approval, he had not taken account of these changes. In addition, he had not consulted the English Church authorities when he answered the call from across the ocean. As a consequence, his first years in Tonga were punctuated by reactions to his presence, from inside and outside the Kingdom, that he interpreted as opposition. Rather than dampening his enthusiasm, this further isolated Willis from the rapid changes taking place in the first decade of the new century, and led to entrenchment of his mid Victorian religious and political attitudes.

CHAPTER THREE - SOURCE NOTES

1 W.P.H. 18/7/1902; Petition to Willis: Nuku'alofa 24/12/1901 (JBP); Willis to Montgomery: Nuku'alofa 16/4/1909 (USPG/CLR/NZ&P/3/319). 2 ACR: 100. 3 ibid.; Willis 1903: 2; Layreader's Licence issued by Alfred Willis to Usaia Kauvaka: Nuku'alofa 5/7/1902 (JBP); Shipping Report Book (National Archives of New Zealand, Auckland C/A/5/3) (hereafter NANZ) 4 ACR: 61, 62, 104. 5 ACR: 51, 100, 103. 6 ACR: 103; Willis 1903: 2. 7 Petition to Willis: Nuku'alofa 24/12/1901 (JBP); Willis 1903: 3; Mark 1960; Mark 1936: 8-10; Trood to Willis: Apia 7/8/1902 (NANZ/Samoan Archives/BCS/7/5/g). 8 See Bibliography 1. Alfred Willis and the Tongan Mission Press for service booklets. 9 Willis 1903: 3. 10 Willis 1919: 4; Charles E. Mathews to Bp. King: Lymington, Hants. 14/11/1920 copy (NAF/DP/DT/5); Mark 1960. 11 Typescript of Willis' Letter to the Supporters...(Willis 1906) (JBP). 12 Episcopal Acts... for 1916 and 1917 (USPG/Missionary Reports 1917/A/50). 13 Willis 1903: 3; Nevill to Abp. of Canterbury: Dunedin 11/3/1904 (USPG/CLR/NZ7P/3/222); Willis to Montgomery: Braceborough 22/11/1912 (USPG/CLR/NZ&P/3/448-449). 14 E.Stiles to Willis: Honolulu 12/12/1907 (JBP). 15 Mark 1960; Mark 1964: 2. 16 Willis to Potts: Nuku'alofa 16/12/1903; ibid. 2/5/1904; Potts to Willis: St John's College, Shanghai 13/2/1904; Willis to Bp of Victoria (Hong Kong): Nuku'alofa 2/5/1904; ibid. 22/10/1905 (NAF/DP/DT/4). 17 Bp.W.F.Nichols to Willis: San Francisco 3/4/1905; ibid.: Mammoth Hot Springs, Yellowstone Nat. Park 20/7/1905; ibid. San Francisco 3/6/1909; Willis to Nichols: Nuku'alofa 11/11/1909 (JBP); Mark 1936: 65; F.T. 28/8/1909. 18 Willis 1911: 3; Willis to Twitchell: Nuku'alofa 4/4/1910 (NAF/DP/DT/3); New Zealand Herald 24/2/1910, 2/3/1910. 19 Mark 1960; Mark 1964: 1; Thomas Trood's Official Diary 1900-1913 entry of 6/7/1906 (NANZ/Samoan Archives/BCS/7/5/g); Bp. Neligan to Sec. of Customs: Auckland 3/3/1910 (Inwards Letter Register NANZ/C/2/11/1910/485); Sec. of Customs to Collector of Customs, Auckland: Wellington 21/3/1910 (Inwards Letter File NANZ/C/A/1/18/1910/398); Y.S. Mark to Willis: Tivoli Hotel, Apia 9/7/1906 (JBP). 20 Willis 1911: 4. 21 Church Gazette of the Diocese of Auckland 1/6/1910; Declaration of Yim Sang Mark to Bishop Alfred Willis 22/5/1910 (JBP). 22 Willis 1913: 4-6. 23 Muir 1951: 330. 24 ibid.; Restarick 1924: 143, 148, 196. 25 V.S. Fox to Willis: C.M.S, London 6/5/1910. 26 Tonga Church Chronicle No.2 (July 1913): 3-4; Muir 1951: 330-333. 27 Layreader's Licence issued by Alfred Willis to Usaia Kauvaka: Nuku'alofa 5/7/1902 (JBP); Tonga Church Chronicle No.2 (July 1913): 2; Lesisita Mali - Vava'u, 1909-1911 Marriage Register for Vava'u (Courthouse, Vava'u). 28 Interview with Kapatoka: Pukotala 25/7/1988; Willis to Montgomery: Nuku'alofa 1/10/1908 (USPG/CLR/NZ&P/3/309A). 29 "Constitution and Canons of the Anglican Church in Tonga"1904, Revised 1906; Koe Konisitutone; Clarke 1924: 195. 30 "Letter to Supporters.. of the Church in Tonga" 11/6/1906 (JBP). 31 Willis 1904 (in Pacific Commercial Advertiser 25/5/1905); Willis 1919: 3. 32 Willis 1903: 2; Willis 1909: 6; Willis to Abp. of Canterbury: Braceborough 31/10/1912 (USPG/CLR/NZ&P/3/446); Willis to Montgomery: Nuku'alofa 30/6/1919 (USPG/CLR/NZ&P/4/92); Revised Edition of the Laws of Tonga 1928: 314. 33 Tonga Church Chronicle No.1 (April 1913): 3, No.2 (July 1913): 2 ; Willis 1904 (in Pacific Commercial Advertiser 25/5/1905); ACR; Willis to W.T.Campbell: Nuku'alofa 17/3/1910. 34 Y.S.Mark to

Hon Sibu, Minister of Lands: Nuku'alofa 2/3/1910; Minisita Fonua ki Bisope Uilisi: Nuku'alofa 18/7/1910 (JBP); Willis 1911: 4. 35 Tonga Church Chronicle No.2 (July 1913): 2; Willis to Hon. J. Sibu: Nuku'alofa 2/3/1909; Sibu to Willis: Nuku'alofa 5/4/1909 (JBP); Willis 1908: 5; Willis 1909: 3; Y.S.Mark to Willis: Vava'u 9/6/1915 (JBP); Willis 1919: 3. 36 Willis to Lowe: Honolulu 18/5/1901 (NAF/DP/DT/3); Willis to Montgomery: Nuku'alofa 30/6/1919 (USPG/CLR/NZ&P/4/92). 37 Letter of Willis to Church Times 19/2/1904; Willis 1905 (in Pacific Commercial Advertiser 25/5/1905); Nevill to Abp. of Canterbury: Dunedin 11/3/1904 (USPG/CLR/NZ&P/3/222); Tonga Church Chronicle No.2 (July 1913): 2; interview with Bp. Fine Halapua: Halaleva 16/3/1988; "Letter to Supporters.. of the Church in Tonga" 11/6/1906 (JBP); Y.S. Mark to Willis: Tivoli Hotel, Apia 9/7/1906 (JBP). 38 Willis 1905 (in Pacific Commercial Advertiser 25/5/1905); Willis 1908: 4. 39 Tonga Government Gazette No.12 (June 1914): 93-102; Willis 1911: 5. 40 E.Stiles to Willis: Honolulu 21/8/1908 (JBP); Tonga Church Chronicle No.3 (Oct.1913): 2-3; Làtūkefu 1974: 124-125. 41 Willis to Abp. of Canterbury: Braceborough 31/10/1912 (USPG/CLR/NZ&P/3/446); ibid./446, /449; Pascoe to Willis: S.P.G., London 3/7/1913 (USPG/CLS/NZ&P/3/25). 42 Willis' Application for S.P.G. support (USPG/OLR/1911-1912/211/50); Willis 1915: 3-4; Willis 1919: 2. 43 Interview with Bp. Fine Halapua: Halaleva 16/3/1988; St Stephen's School Correspondence (including inspectors' reports) 1905-1922 (NANZ/BAAA-1001/1029/b); Willis 1916: 5; Episcopal Acts... for 1916 and 1917 (USPG/Missionary Reports 1917/A/50); ACR: 111-112; annotated notes of Bishop Fine Halapua 30/8/1988. 44 Petition to Willis: Nuku'alofa 24/12/1901 (JBP). 45 Mark 1964: 2; Willis 1909: 2; Willis to Bp of Polynesia: Nuku'alofa 15/9/1909 (NAF/DP/DT/3). 46 W.Osbourne Allen to Abp. of Canterbury: S.P.C.K. (copy) 30/5/1910 (USPG/CLR/NZ&P/3/356); Pascoe to Rev'd A. Shepherd: S.P.G., London 4/6/1910 (USPG/CLS/NZ&P/2/209); Willis 1916: 3; Willis 1919: 3; Pascoe to Willis: S.P.G., London 16/9/1912 (USPG/CLS/NZ&P/3/3). 47 See Bibliography 1. Alfred Willis and the Tongan Mission Press. 48 Willis 1898. 49 Exceptions in Willis 1905 (in Pacific Commercial Advertiser 25/5/1905); Willis 1912: 3. 50 Notes on interview of Mrs Willis by the Rev'd Harold Anson (LPL/FP/Winnigham- Ingram/Willis 1906/148; Willis 1911: 10. 51 USPG/Ledger - Foreign Diocese; 484, 497. 52 Willis' reports, and analysis in Pinson 1970: 93. 53 Willis 1903: 1. 54 F.T. 4/4/1900. 55 Diary extracts by courtesy of Clarence Michalis, New York. 56 Tonga Government Gazette No.12 14/7/1905; Fusitu'a 1976: 175. 57 Interview with Bp. Fine Halapua: Halaleva 2/5/1988; ACR Baptism records; Willis 1911: 5. 58 Interview with Asita Langi: Mangaia 20/9/1988; ACR Baptism records. 59 Y.S. Mark to Willis: Vava'u 9/6/1915 (JBP): interviews with Bp. Fine Halapua: Halaleva 2/5/1988; Karl Tu'inukuafe; Herne Bay, Auckland 24/1/1988; Latai Havili; Kolomotu'a 31/8/1988. 60 Willis to Montgomery: Nuku'alofa 1/10/1908 (USPG/CLR/NZ&P/3/309A); R.T.Mathews report on visit to Tonga (USPG/Missionary Reports/1910/50); Episcopal Acts... for 1916 and 1917 (USPG/Missionary Reports 1917/A/50). 61 Willis 1914: 4; Y.S. Mark to Willis: Vava'u 9/6/1915 (JBP). 62 ACR; Lesisita Pekia - Nuku'alofa Death Register (Courthouse, Nuku'alofa). 63 Cyclopaedia of Tonga 1907: 46-64; Correspondence relating to Affairs in Tonga 1902-1906 : 43-44; Pacific Commercial Advertiser 27/5/1902. 64 e.g.W.P.H. 15/8/1902, 16/9/1902, 2/1/1903; Diary of

Emma Schober 1902-1921: 48 (transcript in German - ref. courtesy of Dr. Kurt During: Kolofo'ou 17/10/1988).65 Twitchell to Montgomery: Suva 22/2/1909 (USPG/OLR/1910-1911/196/58); interview with Ileoraine Pegler: Kolofo'ou 27/4/1988. 66 Episcopal Acts... for 1916 and 1917 (USPG/Missionary Reports 1917/A/50); Handwritten sermon notes (For the "Octave of the Saints") Alfred Willis: n.d. (NAF/DP/DT/3). 67 Willis 1912: 3; ACR: various refs; interview with Ileoraine Pegler: Kolofo'ou 27/4/1988. 68 E.Stiles to Willis: Honolulu 27/5/1908 (JBP); Ellem 1981: 162; Howe 1984: 193; Shipping Report Book (NANZ/C/A/9/1) (NANZ/55-1/111); New Zealand Herald 6/5/1905, 23/9/1910, 24/5/1911, 25/3/1909, 6/1/1906, 26/6/1907: Mrs Willis to Bp. Nevill: Pagnell 20/10/1906 (enclosure in Nevill to Montgomery: London 23/10/1906) (USPG/CLR/NZ&P/2/271). 69 Willis 1916: 4; Mark 1960; Willis to Bp. King (copy) enclosed in King to Twitchell: S.P.G.,London 2/12/1920 (NAF/DP/DT/5). 70 "Letter to Supporters.. of the Church in Tonga" 11/6/1906 (JBP); Willis 1908: 5; ACR: 59; Willis to Montgomery: Nuku'alofa 30/6/1919 (USPG/CLR/NZ&P/4/92). 71 Willis 1914: 4; Y.S. Mark to Willis: Vava'u 9/6/1915 (JBP); Notes taken by writer at a faikava: Hihifo, Lifuka 20/7/1988; Willis 1918: 3; Willis 1919: 2; Lesisita Pekia - Ha'apai 1904-1928 Deaths Register (Courthouse, Pangai). 72 Interview with Lelenoa: Hihifo, Ha'apai 1/8/1988; annotated notes of Bishop Fine Halapua 30/8/1988. 73 "Letter to Supporters.. of the Church in Tonga" 11/6/1906 (JBP); ACR: 63; Willis 1908: 3. 74 "Letter to Supporters.. of the Church in Tonga" 11/6/1906 (JBP); Willis 1908: 4; Willis 1909: 2. 75 Interviews with Sione Palaki & Komiti Kepueli: Mo'unga-one 28/7/1988; Willis to Montgomery: Nuku'alofa 1/10/1908 (USPG/CLR/NZ&P/3/309A). 76 ACR; interview with Sioeli Filihia: Hihifo, Lifuka 20/7/1988; annotated notes of Bishop Fine Halapua 30/8/1988. 77 Willis 1916: 4; Willis 1918:4; Union Steam Ship Company of New Zealand Pocket Guides (Wellington Maritime Museum, Wellington). 78 Lesisita Pekia - Ha'apai 1904-1928 Deaths Register (Courthouse, Pangai); Willis 1916:3; Willis 1918: 3; Willis 1919: 4. 79 "Letter to Supporters.. of the Church in Tonga" 11/6/1906 (JBP); ACR: 101; Episcopal Acts... for 1916 and 1917 (USPG/Missionary Reports 1917/A/50). 80 Interview with Finau Fatai: St Andrew's School, Longolongo 18/3/1988; Interview with Bp. Fine Halapua: Halaleva 16/3/1988; St Stephen's School Correspondence (including inspectors' reports) 1905-1922 (NANZ/BAAA-1001/1029/b). 81 Episcopal Acts... for 1916 and 1917 (USPG/Missionary Reports 1917/A/50). 82 Willis 1912: 4; Willis 1916: 3. 83 ACR: various refs.; Willis to Twitchell: Nuku'alofa 24/3/1909 (NAF/DP/DT/3). 84 Willis 1918: 4; Index of British & Foreign Deaths (Courthouse, Nuku'alofa). 85 Gifford 1924: 281. 86 Latūkefu 1974: 31-32, 119-120, 125-126; Collocott 1921: 156-159; Gifford 1924: 284-285. 87 Whelan 1960: 158, 160-162. 88 Steley 1986. 89.Britsch 1986: 431-436, 446-448. 90 Gifford 1924: 282. 91 Episcopal Acts... for 1916 and 1917 (USPG/Missionary Reports 1917/A/50).

# CHAPTER 4

# ...IN THE FACE OF ALL OPPOSITION

*"East of Fiji, our own branch of the Church provides no  ministration whatever, to either native or settler ... whilst Imperial interests are looked after carefully enough, there has been no corresponding zeal to provide for the spiritual  needs of the isles that stud the ocean." (Willis 1903:1)*

## I

The British Government's relationship with the Kingdom of Tonga in the last quarter of the nineteenth century was complex and often appeared contradictory. Following the annexation of Fiji in 1874, the main thrust was to prevent the influence of any other power on the eastern flank of that colony. Any other relationships which developed were largely incidental to that policy. On the other hand, the intention of both King George Tupou I, and his great grandson who succeeded him in 1893, was to maintain the independence of the Kingdom at almost any cost against the encroachment of any of the great powers, including Britain, as they carved up the Pacific.

King George Tupou I had been assisted in his aims by the Rev'd Shirley Baker from at least 1862, firstly as an unofficial adviser, and between 1880 and 1890, as Premier. Although Baker was motivated by concerns that had more to do with his own personal aggrandisement, Baker was nonetheless energetic in his pursuit to keep Tonga for the Tongans. Baker's actions often incited bitter disputes with the British residents of the Kingdom. In addition to resenting the measures imposed on them by the Tongan Government at Baker's direction, they always suspected Baker of being hand- in-glove with Germany, Britain's principal rival for the favours of Tonga. These conflicts, in which the `beach' community was forced at times into curious alliances with the Wesleyan missionaries and various groups of disaffected hou'eiki, ensured the frequent intervention of the High Commissioner for the Western Pacific in Tongan affairs. This culminated in the order of prohibition served on Baker in May 1890 to facilitate the removal of his dominating influence from the Kingdom.[1]

Upon Baker's departure, the then High Commissioner, Sir John Thurston, appointed one of his Suva staff, Basil Thomson, for one year, to assist in correcting some of the confusion in the Tongan administration that was the legacy of Baker's premiership. After Thomson's work was completed in 1891, there was little direct British involvement in the affairs of the Kingdom in the final decade of the century. The High Commissioner was kept informed of politics in Tonga by the British Vice Consul, R. Beckwith Leefe, who also provided Willis with background information on Baker's Church between 1899 and 1901.[2]

When Britain again asserted her power in early 1900, it was not as the result of any internal problems in the Kingdom, but as a consequence of the final settling of affairs in the South Pacific between the great powers. After a decade of confusion in the Samoan archipelego, Britain, Germany and the United States agreed to restrict their activities in western Polynesia to Tonga, Savai'i and Upolu, and Tutuila respectively. The latter two powers annexed a partitioned Samoa in 1899. A Treaty of Friendship and Protection was 'negotiated' between Britain and Tonga by Basil Thomson and reluctantly signed by King George Tupou II on 18th May, 1900.[3]

Under the Treaty, the King undertook to enter into relations with no other power except Britain, and the status of British representation in Tonga was raised to Agent and Consul. This official was given jurisdiction over all foreign residents, and although he was to have no right to interfere in internal affairs, he would give 'advice' when requested. Annexation was considered inevitable by most of those in the Colonial Office, including Basil Thomson. However the Western Pacific High Commission Staff were anxious to protect the Kingdom from "the tender mercies of Seddon... [and] his New Zealand Parliamentary hoodlums." *(Scarr 1967:110)* Seddon desired a South Pacific empire and was sore over missing out in the partition of Samoa in 1899. He believed that he had been promised Tonga as compensation by certain officials in the Colonial Office, and visited the Kingdom soon after the signing of the 1900 Treaty. Seddon fostered a relationship with the King, who was still bitter over being pressured into a protectorate relationship with Britain. Baker, in typical style, encouraged these overtures with an eye to favours from the New Zealand Government.[4]

With the upgrading of British representation, Leefe retired in late 1900, and was replaced in February 1901. The new British Agent and Consul was W. Hamilton Hunter who, it was considered by British officials, would be better able to put the King's vanity to good use.[5] One of Hunter's first acts was to attempt to exchange the existing British residency for Baker's former residence, which stood on a larger 'api known as Mala'e'aloa closer to the

Royal Palace. This was occupied by Edmund Lowe, a brother-in-law of Emil Hutter, of the Auckland firm of Hutter Brothers, who had virtually monopolised Tongan Government business since Baker's commercial demise. The matter was not settled to the Agent and Consul's satisfaction until a visit of the *H.M.S. Torch* in September 1901. The cavalier attitude of Hunter in his frequent representations to the King and High Commissioner over Mala'e'aloa, and on behalf of European residents on a plethora of petty concerns, aggravated King George Tupou II. This pushed the King and Sateki, his Premier, further in the welcoming arms and extended credit of the Hutter Brothers.[6]

It was into this atmosphere of understandable mistrust of British designs that the Willises landed in Nuku'alofa in June 1902, their arrival coinciding with one of the frequent visits of the *H.M.S. Torch* as a show of British strength.[7] Basil Thomson, in a move of uncharacteristic sensitivity, had earlier advised Willis that he felt it would be inappropriate, given the resentment over the 1900 Treaty, for there seen to be British aggression in matters ecclesiastical as well as political. Thomson believed that it would be better to wait until after the inevitable annexation of the Kingdom by Britain to establish the Anglican Church.[8]

Willis' close relationship with British officials was already known to the King, from the events and correspondence of early 1900, as was his offer to make the Anglican Church the National Church of Tonga. Willis was aware that his actions were potentially open to misinterpretation, and in addition, he knew that in accepting the call of the former followers of Baker, who included members of the 'Ofa-ki-Vava'u `party', he was doing so against the advice of the King.[9] These factors, complicated by the recent involvement of Polutele Kaho, did not bode well for his reception in official Tongan circles.

Willis was accustomed to opposition to his almost every move in Honolulu, and believed that the Anglican Church members were being persecuted in his first years in Tonga due to this complex mixture of internal and external factors. He cited as examples threats by the King to deprive Polutele of the title and tofi'a of Tu'ivakanō that he was due to inherit, as a result of his continued involvement as Willis' interpreter. Willis also believed that Thomas Rudling, the Postmaster and Sub-Collector of Customs at Neiafu, an associate of Willis from Honolulu (who accidentally introduced the *pi kula* - red wasp to Tonga with some beehives from Hawai'i), had been threatened with dismissal in November 1902 if he lodged Willis in his house. Willis considered that many more would join the Church if it were not for their fear of the King.[10] Difficult to confirm, these allegations by Willis were more likely a rationalisation for the failure of the Tongans to instantly respond to his fuller Christianity. Whilst a milestone for Alfred Willis, the establishment of the Anglican Church was a non-event for those outside its tiny circle, and drew little official comment.[11]

There was little doubt that Willis' close identification with the British cause did not assist him in his efforts to gain land leases for his Church. These requests, like those of the committee of British residents keen to build a hall in Nuku'alofa as a memorial to Queen Victoria, were met with offers of land outside the town area.[12] His close association with the meddling Hunter and other British officials, would have done little to raise his stakes with the King and Government.

Willis' contacts with the Western Pacific High Commission hierarchy however remained informal, being the result of his natural involvement as an Anglican bishop, rather than any formal political representation. His conveniently timed visit to Fiji in mid 1904, during the crisis leading up to the Christmas coup d'etat of that year in Tonga, could be seen in that light. It was hardly likely that the Acting High Commissioner, Sir Charles Major, and Willis would have only discussed the niceties of ecclesiastical polity during the ten days which the Bishop and Mrs Willis spent as guests at the Vice Regal Residence in Suva in July.[13]

Willis' contacts in high places eventually paid off. The new High Commissioner, Sir Everard im Thurn, deposed the Government in December 1904, and replaced the entire Cabinet, except Fatafehi Tu'ipelehake, the King's father, with ministers of his own choosing. The Anglican Church was one of those groups selected for special mention in regard to the granting of leases to foreigners in the Kingdom.[14] Willis made it quite clear that he approved of im Thurn's action in "stopping the leak in the Treasury safe ... [and] ending the occupation of the Jew [the Hutter Brothers]." *(Willis 1905 in Pacific Commercial Advertiser 25/5/1905)* Willis was granted the first of his land leases in early 1905.

Polutele's role in both the Anglican Church and as a pro-British protagonist were part of his path to the premiership which he achieved by the end of Willis' first decade in Tonga. His career had taken a definite turn for the worst with his dismissal as private secretary to the Premier in 1900, for insubordination. His reputation for being outspoken had made him unpopular with many in government circles.[15] His close involvement with Willis could be seen as a means of regaining some standing. There was no doubt that Willis was pleased with the `young chief'[16] (Polutele was thirty two in 1902) who gave potential status to his Church. This was particularly so when Taemanusa and Tevita Ula Afuha'amango left the Church in 1904.

Polutele was due to succeed to the title and tofi'a of Tu'ivakanō on the death of Manoa, the present holder. Manoa had no legitimate male descendant entitled to succeed. Therefore the title would go to the next in line of descent of Mataele Tu'apiko, their common ancestor, this other line having held the title until Manoa's succession in 1888. They had been passed over because Manatua, the previous holder, and a half-brother of Polutele's mother, 'Ana Kaho, was supposed illegitimate. As there were no other male heirs in this line, Polutele, as 'Ana's eldest son, would succeed. When Polutele died in 1923 without issue, his brother Siosiua succeeded. This was challenged in the Land Court by Molitoni Finau, on behalf of his son Lupeti, a great grandson of Manoa who had been born after Polutele's succession, on the grounds of Manatua's alleged illegitimacy. The Court ruled for Siosiua, the charge being unable to be sustained.[17]

The action of the King and Privy Council in applying pressure on Polutele, which included a threat to disinherit him, in an effort to force him to end his arrangement with Mrs Krause to occupy the key trading site in Kolofo'ou desired by the Hutter Brothers, had pushed him further into the pro-British camp. Agent and Consul Hunter saw Polutele as a potential leader of Tongan opposition to the King and Sateki. The `Mrs Krause affair' was settled with a further visit of the *H.M.S. Torch* some two months before im Thurn's coup d'etat.[18] Polutele's further submissions to the Agent and Consul, and his action, as the first to speak out against the King and Premier at a meeting called by im Thurn when he arrived in December 1904, were catalysts in the resulting humiliation of the Government. Polutele was rewarded for his efforts with the post of minister in the new Cabinet formed by im Thurn on 16th January 1905.[19]

Now secure in his position, and continuing to keep his links with Hunter and im Thurn, he married Kilisitina, whose family were leaders in the Kolofo'ou congregation. Curiously, his confirmation as an Anglican was delayed until 1909.[20]

Polutele's sympathies with the British were stretched during the term of W. Telfer Campbell as British Agent and Consul from September 1909 to February 1912. Campbell's insensitive handling of all matters, and especially his involvement in the `Kautaha Toga ma'a Toga affair' in 1910 lost the Agent and Consul the support of even Alfred Willis.

Polutele was installed as Tu'ivakanō in March 1912, and then in October of the same year, whilst Willis was in England, he was appointed Premier. He replaced Mateialona, whom im Thurn had made Premier in 1905, and who had resigned in the recriminations which followed Campbell's demise. Tu'ivakanō had attempted to have the King deposed and replaced by the monarch's father, Fatafehi Tu'ipelehake, in 1905, and probably was not the King's first choice as his chief minister. But his obvious abilities were recognised by King George Tupou II as they had been by Willis and the British officials. His ministry marked a new chapter in the relationship between Tonga and Britain, and both Tupou II and the young Queen Salote who succeeded her father in 1918, enjoyed a more equitable status with their powerful protector.[21]

Polutele Tu'ivakanō's prominent role in the Anglican Church ended in 1912, although he and Kilisitina continued to maintain a close personal relationship with the Willises. The Bishop lost his best educated and highest ranking member, whose decision to cease public involvement in the Church had obvious political motivations, in common with most of his actions of the preceding decade. The defection of Taemanusa and Tevita Ula Afuha'amango in 1904 had resulted in a considerable drop in membership of the Kolofo'ou congregation. In contrast, Polutele had never led a 'party' within the Church, his actions in the religious sphere, as in politics, being pragmatic and opportunist.

Although his personal sympathies continued to lie with Willis and the Anglicans, he did not live long enough to lead a movement to swell the numbers of the Anglican ranks during the religious upheavals of the mid 1920s. He died in 1923 of tuberculosis, his funeral being conducted by the Rev'd Jabez Watkin. Kilisitina then resumed a leading role in the Kolofo'ou congregation which she maintained until her death in 1971.[22]

With or without Polutele Tu'ivakanō's involvement, Willis looked to British rather than traditional structures, to legitimise the activities of his Church. Two examples of this were the opening of the schools built by Willis. In 1905 Sir Everard im Thurn opened the first building erected on the Kolofo'ou 'api, and similarly, St. Andrew's School was opened in April 1914 by the then British Agent and Consul, H.E.W. Grant.[23] In return, the British officials employed Willis, rather than other Church leaders, to celebrate their major civic events, such as the coronation of Edward VII in August 1902. This was followed "in the evening by a select party at the British consulate."

Edward VII's death were similarly conducted by Willis, the King and Queen Takipo attending.[24] This set a precedent for Anglican relationships with others in the Tongan community. The membership of the Anglican Church were seen by many as a pro-British elite, but in common with most other denominational differences in the Kingdom, other Church groups reacted with indifference rather than antagonism.[25]

Willis' arrival in the Kingdom to establish his fuller Christianity went almost unnoticed by the head of the religious group of which Willis was most critical. The Rev'd Jabez Watkin, as president of the Siasi Tau'ataina, was aware of Willis' links with Baker and 'Ofa-ki-Vava'u, and his ambitions to make the Anglican Church the National Church of Tonga, through his close relationship with the King as Royal chaplain and as his unofficial adviser. Watkin saw little threat from the ageing Willis.[26] Here again, it was Willis who set up the situation ready for response, but unlike Honolulu, where there were plenty of opponents, both Anglican and Congregationalist, ready to pick a fight, Willis made little impact outside his circle of followers. He saw his mission in far grander terms than it was perceived by his so-called opponents.

The Wesleyan Mission were the only religious group to make any significant response to Willis' intention to `consummate' what he saw as the `inadequate' form of Christianity that the Tongans had received. Some two years before his arrival in Tonga, the *Australasian Methodist Missionary Review* of 6th June 1900 carried the full text of Willis' effusive pastoral letter to 'Ofa-ki-Vava'u of February 1900. In an article entitled "Ignorance or Impertinence" the writer expressed disgust at `We, Alfred's' insinuations that the Tongans had received a deficient form of Christianity from the Wesleyan missionaries. He was quick to point out that Tongan missionaries had been responsible for taking the Christian gospel to many other Pacific Islands. However it was felt that the Tongans "may be trusted to take care of themselves" and the writer dismissed Willis' letter as "almost too benighted and silly to deserve further comment".

Dr. Moulton, as chairman of the Tonga District, did not see Willis' work as a real threat to any other denomination in Tonga, but felt it necessary to lodge a formal protest to the Anglican authorities. A resolution passed at the General Conference of the Methodist Church held in Melbourne in May 1904 was forwarded to various bishops.[27]

The establishment of Willis' mission in Tonga was seen as breaking the comity that had existed between the Protestant missions dating from the

1850s. Bishop G.A. Selwyn had claimed the vast unoccupied Melanesian field for his Melanesian Mission, beginning work in 1849. Through lack of finance and an unusual missionary technique, the progress had been slow. The Wesleyans, who had worked in New Britain and New Ireland since the 1870s, moved eastwards into the Western Solomon Islands in 1902 with the reluctant agreement of the Bishop of Melanesia, Cecil Wilson. A copy of the General Conference resolution was sent to Wilson, who was unsympathetic to the Wesleyan concern over Willis' entry into Tonga, resenting the 'intrusion' into his own area of influence in the Solomon Islands.[28] These discussions had little impact on Willis' work in Tonga, or his relationships with the local missionaries or Siasi Fakaongo members, as he did not recognise the so-called Selwyn Compact.

## II

Of much more concern to Willis was the lack of recognition of his work in Tonga by the Church of England, under whose banner he was attempting to establish the Church true and Catholic in the Kingdom.

The Anglican authorities in London used the Selwyn compact and their sensitivity over the embarrassingly slow progress of the Melanesian Mission, as an excuse to attempt to thwart Willis' ambitions in Tonga.[29] Ever since the Willises' had visited the South Pacific in 1897, Willis had considered himself as Bishop of Oceana (for some unknown reason *Oceana* not *Oceania* was used in all the correspondence on this matter), and had received encouragement in this from the veteran William Floyd in Levuka, and his family and friends in England. William Lowe, a solicitor and first cousin of Willis, had been treasurer of the Hawai'ian Mission Association since 1887 and was closely involved in most of his projects, including fundraising for Floyd's memorial church in Levuka and the Samoa campaign. Lowe had been unafraid to use his contacts with Lord Stanmore (formerly Sir Arthur Gordon) at the British Colonial Office in the past to promote Willis' ambitions in Samoa and Tonga. He approached the overworked Bishop of London in 1900 and 1901 to release his jurisdiction over the South Pacific to enable Willis to act in his stead, not as a commissary, but as an extra- provincial bishop.[30]

Here Willis came up against the newly appointed secretary of the Society for the Propagation of the Gospel in Foreign Parts., Bishop H.H. Montgomery, who was determined to prevent the autocratic Alfred acting as an autocephalous bishop in the South Seas. Montgomery knew the whole messy story of Willis' Honolulu episcopate, and desired to protect an unsuspecting flock in Tonga, or anywhere else in the South Pacific, from his episcopal activities. In this Montgomery was consistent with the policy of his predecessor, Henry W. Tucker, who had resisted all attempts by Willis to extend his area of influence in the Pacific.[31] Montgomery acted as an adviser to both the new Bishop of London, A.F. Winnington Ingram, and two successive Archbishops of Canterbury, the elderly Frederick Temple, and then Randall Davidson. The latter was noted for his patience and diplomacy, attributes certainly needed when dealing with one so determined as Alfred Willis.

Willis, who had lambasted the S.P.G. for their premature withdrawal of his Honolulu grant in 1900, had no real desire to be subject again to their whims.[32] He realised that his chance of a grant from the Society for his work in Tonga was unlikely with Montgomery at the helm, and made no direct contact with the S.P.G. between 1902 and 1908. He left his cousin William Lowe and his friend Bishop S.T. Nevill to fight the battles on his behalf.

The association of Willis and Nevill went back some thirty years. They had both been consecrated for work in taking the Anglican Church to far flung corners of the globe at about the same year, sharing an interest in extending the work of the Church true and Catholic to the South Pacific. Nevill had licensed Baker as a layreader in 1900, an action which Willis considered foolish in the extreme, but in the storm which broke upon Willis' arrival in Tonga, Nevill turned out to be his only episcopal supporter.[33]

Alfred Willis' request for recognition from the Church of the Province of New Zealand had only a polite acknowledgement from the ailing Primate, Bishop Cowie. The letter was passed to the Senior Bishop and Acting Primate, who happened to be none other than Nevill! He recognised Willis immediately and without consultation as `Missionary Bishop in Tonga'. For his unilateral action, Nevill, who was not popular with the rest of the New Zealand bench and who had earlier earned their rebuke for his licensing of Baker as a layreader, put himself even further out of favour. At a meeting of the bishops held in Auckland in May 1903, they effectively dissociated themselves from Nevill's' commission and withdrew their recognition of Willis. Nevill was unable to agree to this action, and dissented from two of the six resolutions which the bench forwarded to the Archbishop of Canterbury.[34] Despite this further rebuke, Nevill continued to publicly support Willis in New Zealand with frequent publication of Willis' letters and his own articles of support in the monthly newspaper of the Diocese of Dunedin, *The New Zealand Guardian*.[35]

The nett effect of the action of both the English and New Zealand Churches was to leave Willis as self-styled `Missionary Bishop in Tonga', although he wisely, after the `Parnell Resolutions' of 1903, Willis refrained from using this title. This left the field wide open for Nevill to pursue his new role as self-appointed advocate for Willis. Not only did Montgomery hold Nevill in contempt on a level with Willis, for "tactlessness and lack of common sense" *(Memo, 16/3/1903 by Montgomery on letter of Nevill LPL/DP/430/110-116)* but his exaggerated reports on Willis' work, the frequent submissions to Montgomery, the Bishop of London and the Archbishop of Canterbury, did little to further the case of Willis and his Tongan Mission. Nevill made himself even more unpopular with the English Church authorities for encouraging Willis to visit Fiji, and received a gentle rap on the knuckles from the Bishop of London for doing so.[36]

Once resident in Tonga, Willis considered himself to be the Bishop of Oceana, and believed that Nuku'alofa was not only more central than the suggested Fijian base, but also afforded a better working climate for Europeans. Willis made his first, and last, attempt to exercise the authority he did not in fact possess, in June 1904, when he consecrated the Church of the Holy Redeemer in Levuka at William Floyd's request. Willis also conducted confirmations in Levuka and Suva.[37]

Mrs Emma Willis, although unhappy in her situation in Nuku'alofa, nonetheless attempted to gain recognition for her husband's work. In addition to often spending time with the Nevills on her frequent visits to New Zealand, she canvassed on his behalf with the Rev'd Harold Anson, Warden of St. John's College in Auckland, who was considered to be a man of some influence in English Church circles. With Nevills' assistance, she made contact with Montgomery whilst she was in England in 1906.[38] As it turned out, her advocacy in England came at the very time that a decision was made on episcopal jurisdiction in the South Pacific.

Largely through Nevill's persistence, and a desire on the part of the remainder of the New Zealand bench, and the English authorities , that Willis *not* be Diocesan Bishop of Oceana, the Bishop of London and the Archbishop of Canterbury agreed in 1906 to establish the Diocese of Polynesia to be based on Suva. They desired that a younger man with no connection with the Bishop of Dunedin be appointed. They realised however that efforts to move Willis out of Tonga would be if not fruitless, then at least unpleasant. It was agreed that he should stay there for his lifetime if he so desired.[39]

As a result of the advocacy of the Bishop of London, the S.P.G. provided a small grant to Willis from the beginning of 1909, in recognition of his chaplaincy to the English residents of Tonga. Although he was grateful for the tacit recognition of his work that this grant gave, he found it difficult to disguise his disappointment at the paltry sum of one hundred pounds annually.[40] But he did not allow this to prevent building up a warm and close relationship with Montgomery and the other S.P.G. staff in the years which followed. They endured with good natured humour the frequent pious homilies from Willis on the use of alcohol, the dangers of juvenile smoking, the threat of theosophy and a host of other subjects. One particularly lengthy epistle during wartime austerity prompted Montgomery to tactfully reply;
"It is very interesting to hear the views of one so wise in so many directions as yourself... it may comfort you to know how enormously luxuries of the very type [tobacco and wine] have almost been eliminated." *(Montgomery to Willis: S.P.G., London 19/10/1917 USPG/CLS/NZ&P/3/111)*

The result of the six years of silence involving Willis had the opposite effect from that which the English Church authorities had expected. Rather than starving Willis out, it had entrenched his power and authority in Tonga. Accustomed as he was to running his own operation in Hawai'i, he became, by default, an autocephalous (himself the head) bishop in Tonga. As such, autocephalous bishops cannot exist in the Anglican Church, all bishops and dioceses not included in a province being responsible to the Archbishop of Canterbury. Throughout the discussions in the Church regarding Willis' entry into Tonga, there was never any question about the validity of his orders or consecration, and he was not regarded as *episcopi vagantes* (wandering bishop) in the later sense of the word. He rather had parallels with those wandering bishops who disrupted Church order in continental Europe during early medieval times.[41]

Willis' continuing independent nature was demonstrated when Thomas Clayton Twitchell was consecrated and installed as the first Bishop of the vast and watery Diocese of Polynesia in 1908. Instructed to leave Willis well alone, he visited briefly in early 1909, following which he and Willis engaged in lengthy arguments by letter over Willis' title and legal status in the diocese, which had shades of the Honolulu controversies. Only too glad to have one corner of his impossible jurisdiction catered for, he was not prepared to concede titles suggested by Willis which would have effectively created a new diocese within his own.[42] The diplomatic intervention of Archbishop Davidson, to whom Twitchell had appealed, eventually settled the matter to the satisfaction of both men, and Willis received a commission as Assistant Bishop for Tonga on 13th July 1913. He was then able to take his rightful place amongst those listed in the Church almanacs, and not amongst those whom he described as being `turned out to grass' *(Willis to Nevill: Nuku'alofa 28/3/1911).*[43]

With or without a commission, Willis saw himself as the Bishop of Tonga, and inclusion in the Diocese of Polynesia made no practical difference to his work. In his later years, he made plans to extend the jurisdiction he did not in fact possess, to include Samoa, Niue and the Cook Islands. He was initially encouraged in this by his work amongst the Niuean community at Halafo'ou. Kathleen Howard, who had worked as a missionary-teacher in Aitutaki, joined her family at Tonga College in 1910. She brought with her a young man from the Cook Islands by the name of Tangitoru Ngativaru. It was said that he wished to become an Anglican priest.[44] He married a Tongan named Meleane Fehoko and taught at St. Andrew's School in 1915. When he was unable to carry on through ill health, Ngativaru was replaced by another Cook Islander, Harry Terapo. Terapo also married a Tongan and continued to teach at St. Andrew's School until 1923, when he moved to 'Eua. Willis was pleased to have a potential opening in Eastern Polynesia through these two men, and he made plans to translate the Prayer Book into Rarotongan.[45] It is unclear whether he ever began the project.

Willis was overjoyed when he read in the *Auckland Weekly News* of 18th June 1914 that the London Missionary Society were likely to withdraw from part of their Pacific work in an effort to reduce costs. This was another example of the long awaited disintegration of the Nonconformists which he had cited amongst his reasons for the urgency to establish the Anglican Church in Samoa in 1897. Willis wanted to be ready to fill any vacuum to be left by the proposed withdrawal of the L.M.S. missionaries. Despite attempts by Montgomery to dampen his enthusiasm for an Eastern Polynesian diocese, Willis, who had already publicly announced in 1912 that it was his intention to endow a new see to be based on Nuku'alofa in his will, persisted with this idea to the end of his life.[46]

# III

Alfred Willis believed that the presence of the Anglican Church in the Kingdom of Tonga was for the good of all, including those outside its tiny membership. He noted in 1908 a general improvement not just between the Anglicans and the membership of other Churches, but also between the two rival forms of lotu Uesiliana. He put this down to the good influence of his Anglican Church. Whilst this sentiment of co-operation was echoed by others in the same period, there were more important factors at work in the Kingdom which had brought about the gradual improvement in relationships than the presence of Alfred Willis or his Church true and Catholic.

A number of the protagonists of the controversies of the 1880s had died or mellowed their views over the intervening years. Watkin's *bete noire*, the talented Dr. J.E. Moulton, had retired as chairman of the Tongan District in 1905. Watkin's view of the Fakaongo had tempered as a result, especially after 1908, when the Rev'd Rodger Page arrived from Australia to head the Wesleyan work. Page was universally liked, and his abilities as a raconteur enjoyed, even in Watkin's own home.[47] This improving situation enabled the leaders of these three Churches to co-operate on at least two projects at the end of Willis' first decade in Tonga.

From at least December 1910, Page had been concerned about the actions of the new British Agent and Consul, W. Telfer Campbell, who was turning out to be even more meddlesome than his predecessor. Hunter had retired in September 1909, despite a petition from the European residents of Nuku'alofa that he remain in the job. Campbell's' arrogant, insensitive and patronising approach to Tongans and Europeans alike, soon lost him favour. An example of his unpopularity was indivcated by the efforts of the committee of the Queen Victoria Memorial Hall to remove the rule that the Agent and Consul be ex officio on that committee![48]

Matters were brought to head during the 'Kautaha Toga ma'a Tonga' affair of 1910 - 1911, which Campbell was considered by many to have incited. Willis, Page and Watkin petitioned the High Commissioner on various concerns in the Kingdom, which ranged across topics including the complex matters surrounding the Kautaha case, the interference of Campbell in Cabinet meetings, the state of roads in the Kingdom and the tax imposed on breeding horses! Willis delivered this document in person to the Western Pacific High Commissioner, Sir Francis May, in Suva in July 1911. The High Commissioner questioned the mandate of these Church leaders to speak for the people of Tonga, and was not pleased with what he considered to be their questioning of the authority and integrity of the British officials in both Nuku'alofa and Suva.[49]

The King also made representation to Sir Francis May in September that same year, annoyed at attempts by Campbell to remove his Chief Justice, Robert Skeen, removed from his job. Skeen, who had been appointed to the Cabinet by im Thurn in 1905, was a regular member of Willis' congregation, and had been reasonably successful at blocking Campbell's interference in Cabinet's meetings.[50] When Campbell was recalled in March 1912, the Tonga correspondent for the *Fiji Times*, who was normally biased towards the British standpoint, wrote; "very few will be sorry at his departure" *(op.cit. 14/3/1912)*

In the same year as these Church leaders co-operated in the political arena they also worked together in an effort to counter the efforts of the Latter Day Saints missionaries, who had arrived in Tongatapu from Vava'u in March 1911. From his Hawai'ian experience, Willis held the L.D.S. in utter contempt, and prepared a pamphlet in Tongan to counter their `pernicious tracts'. With the assistance of Page and Watkin, three thousand copies were printed and distributed. It would appear that their campaign made little impact; it certainly did not upset the L.D.S. emissaries, who were accustomed to such reaction, and their membership soon outstripped that of the Anglicans.[51]

The year 1912 was a watershed for Willis. He had effectively silenced criticism from the English Church authorities, and the other Church leaders and the Royal Household had turned from indifference to co-operation. Whilst membership of his Church had not increased, Willis had completed the organisation to his satisfaction, and with the ordination of Filipe Vea early in 1912, provided the three fold ministry he had long desired for Tonga. He now felt secure enough in his position in the Kingdom to leave its shores for an extended period.

He had not left the Pacific since his return from the Lambeth Conference in 1897, and had matters  personal, ecclesiastical and political to which he wished to attend.[52] The Willises" itinerary read like a list of Willis' former adversaries which he systematically checked off. Here at last was a vindication of his actions in responding to the call to Tonga, with all its consequences, real and imagined. After fifteen years, the villain of the piece dared to show his face in the corridors of power. Much to everyone's surprise, he did not turn out to be the ogre that they had imagined. Their trip was a lap of triumph on a global scale!

The Willises travelled initially to Suva, where they awaited passage to Honolulu to join in the celebration of the jubilee of the founding of the Reformed Catholic Church of Hawai'i. In Honolulu, the couple were toasted by the Church membership, the old animosities having been set aside, if not forgotten. The irony of Alfred Willis' presence at the opening of the completed tower of St. Andrew's Cathedral in memory of Alice Mackintosh, the wife of the Rev'd Alexander Mackintosh, could not however have been lost on those present with personal experience of the bitter disputes surrounding the Second Congregation. Willis also took stock of his personal business involvements in the Territory, and gained the estimated value of the considerable property which he still owned in the Honolulu area, which included the bulk of his former Iolani College site.[53]

From Hawai'i the Willises travelled across Canada and on to England, where Willis was able to come face to face with the English Church authorities. He had interviews with Montgomery at the S.P.G., the Bishop of London and the Archbishop of Canterbury.[54] Montgomery wrote to Bishop Twitchell in Suva; "We found Willis quite charming, not in the least difficult, and indeed, very critical of the Bishop of Dunedin, which is the last thing we expected." *(op.cit.    S.P.G.,    London    5/12/1912 USPG/CLS/NZ&P/3/21)*

Whilst in England, Willis arranged for the publication of the new edition of his Tongan Prayer Book with the S.P.C.K. He took every opportunity to publicise his work in Tonga through missionary meetings, and took advice from one S.P.G. staff member on how to "reach people's hearts (and pockets) through letters to the Press." *(Pascoe to Willis: S.P.G., London 19/11/1912 USPG/CLS/NZ&P/3/19)*

Such activities could be expected from the founder of the Anglican Church in Tonga, visiting England, as he was, for the first time in fifteen years. More surprising was his role as a messenger for the King of Tonga, delivering letters from both His Majesty and Tungī Mailefihi to Basil Thomson at the Home Office, requesting that the provisions imposed on the Tongan Government in 1905 by im Thurn be withdrawn. Willis pointed out to Thomson that he considered Campbell to have been the cause of recent problems in the relationship between Britain and the Tongan Government. Thomson however believed that the Colonial Office was unlikely to overturn this 'Supplementary Treaty' whilst its author, Sir Everard im Thurn, was still holding a key position in that department of the British Government.[55] As it turned out, a new era was already beginning with the temporary appointment of Islay McOwan as British Agent and Consul, and Polutele Tu'ivakanō's appointment as the new Premier.

Willis' support for the King in this matter was, at first sight, rather curious given his earlier attitude to the coup d'etat of Christmas 1904. But his involvement with Page and Watkin in attempting to have Campbell removed had probably opened his eyes. The dismissive treatment he had received from Sir Francis May when delivering the petition in 1911 had shown to him that the British officials, whom he had always trusted implicitly, were motivated by expediency rather than a sense of `fair play'. He therefore had been forced to rethink im Thurn's precipitate action in replacing the Cabinet and threatening to depose the King.

Willis was now acting as a loyal subject to his adopted monarch, in relaying the King's feelings to those in England whom he hoped may be able to correct the injustices of the past decade. Willis had at last achieved a workable alliance with the Royal household, something that he had desired since his initial contacts with Baker's Church in 1900. Too little, and too late, he had in some small measure the Royal recognition for his work that he believed was his right as a bishop in the Church true and Catholic, even if this was only as a Royal messenger.

After spending some four months in England, the Willises again crossed the Atlantic and on through the United States to San Francisco. Here they stayed with Bishop Nichols, who had organised the final transfer of the Honolulu diocese to the Protestant Episcopal Church in 1902, and provided for Sang Mark's theological education. From San Francisco they sailed via Tahiti and Rarotonga to Wellington, New Zealand, where Willis, never slow to pick up on a chance for publicity, agreed to be interviewed. This report was carried by a number of important New Zealand daily newspapers.[56]

The aim of their visit to the Dominion was twofold. Firstly it was an opportunity to spend some time with Nevill in Dunedin. These two elders of the Church, of such similar temperament and outlook had actually not met during the fifteen years they shared a common interest in the Church in Tonga. What passed between them can only be speculation, but no more letters from Nevill on Willis' behalf appeared at the S.P.G. in London after this meeting. Having at last built up a good relationship with the Society staff, Willis was presumably not prepared to see this destroyed by Nevill's further interference.

The second reason for Willis' presence in New Zealand was to attend, at

Nevill's personal invitation as Primate, the session of the General Synod of the Province to be held at Nelson in late January 1913. Following a series of speaking engagements in Dunedin city churches, the Willises travelled north to Nelson and the Synod.[57]

The bench of bishops that Willis met bore little resemblance to that which had censured Nevill so strongly in 1903 and at subsequent General Synods for his support of Willis. Only Nevill and Bishop Julius of Christchurch remained. Willis received a polite welcome and was invited to address the gathering on his work in Tonga. He took no part in the formal discussions of the General Synod, Nevill being astute enough to recognise that to do so would be to open up new areas of dissension.[58]

Thus ended their remarkable tour, with Alfred Willis in triumph over all his opposition, however much of this had been in his own mind. He and Mrs Willis returned to Tonga at the end of January 1913, having been absent from the Kingdom for over nine months. Shortly after their arrival, the country suffered a severe hurricane for the second year in a row.[59] The reality of their precarious existence on low, flat coral islands must have rapidly deflated the Willises after the heady heights of their grand tour. They were blissfully unaware of what lay in store for them over the next seven years when much of Willis' Church gradually disintegrated due to the complex interaction of the erratic climate of the Kingdom, the effects of the First World War, the deaths and defections of key leadership, and the disastrous effect of the 1918 mahaki faka'auha on his organisation.

Alfred Willis was now seventy seven years old; his health, and particularly his hearing, deteriorating. He may have silenced his imaginary critics, and established the presence of the Anglican Church in Polynesia, but the future of the Anglican Church in Tonga, where all power and authority, spiritual and temporal, were focused in his person, looked uncertain.

# CHAPTER FOUR - SOURCE NOTES

1 Scarr 1967: 82, 96-107; Rutherford 1971: 63-63, 76, 98, 155-169; Lātūkefu 1975: 43, 56-63.
2 Scarr 1967: 108-109; Rutherford 1971: 170-171. 3 Thomson 1902: 167; Thomson 1937:
202ff; Lātūkefu 1975: 70. 4 The Honourable R.J. Seddon's Visit to the South Seas 1900: 6-62;
Baker to Seddon: Fakapale 4/9/1900 (Seddon Papers - quoted in Cummins 1972: 507-508). 5 Sir
C.T.M. O'Brien to J. Chamberlain, Sec. of State for the Colonies: Suva 22/2/1901 (quoted in
Fusitu'a 1976: 120). 6 Fusitu'a 1976: 97, 121-122, 124-125. 7 F.T. 18/7/1902, 21/7/1902;
Fusitu'a 1976: 134. 8 Thomson to Willis: London 19/10/1900 (JBP). 9 Willis to Nevill:
Nuku'alofa 19/7/1902 (quoted in New Zealand Guardian 1/10/1902). 10 Willis 1903: 2-3; J.
Whitcombe to R. Page: Bayswater, Auckland 21/4/1956 (Pacific Manuscript Bureau Microfilm
634). 11 Interview with 'Eseta Fusitu'a: Kolofo'ou 1/11/1988. 12 Willis 1903: 3. 13 F.T.
13/7/1904; Willis 1905 (in Pacific Commercial Advertiser 25/5/1905). 14 Annextures to the
Report of the High Commissioner to the Western Pacific on the events in the Tonga Islands
December 1904 and January 1905: 41-43. 15 Lavaka 1981: 73; Fusitu'a 1976: 126; Tu'ivakanō
n.d.:3. 16 Willis 1903: 2-3. 17 Tongan Law Reports Vol.II 1963: 13-16. 18 Fusitu'a 1976: 127.
19 im Thurn 1905: 5, 11. 20 Lavaka 1981: 135-138; Tohi 1972: 64; ACR: 108. 21 Lavaka
1981: 159- 229; Lātūkefu 1975: 74-75. 22 Tohi 1972: 40; F.T. 13/6/1921; interviews with Bp.
Fine Halapua: Halaleva 2/5/1988 and Tupou Fanua: Kolofo'ou 26/1/1989; Lesiseta Pekia -
Nuku'alofa Death Register (Courthouse, Nuku'alofa). 23 Tonga Church Chronicle No.2 (July
1913): 4; Mission Field Sept.1915: 281. 24 Western Pacific Herald 12/7/1910; Tonga
Government Gazette No.18 28/5/1910. 25 Decktor Korn 1978: 407-408; Interview with 'Eseta
Fusitu'a: Kolofo'ou 1/11/1988. 26 Lavaka 1981: 32; Fusitu'a 1976: 157, 161. 27 F.T.
12/11/1902 - reprint of article in Sydney Daily Telegraph of 18/10/1902; Methodist Church in
Australasia -Report of the First General Conference 1904: 58-59 "Tongan Affairs-resolutions
9&10". 28 Correspondence between Dr. George Brown and Bp. Cecil Wilson 31/3/1905 &
14/4/1905 (USPG/CLR/NZ&P/3/253E). 29 Notes of Bp. Montgomery on a letter from Bp.
Neligan (LPL/DP/430/123-124). 30 Willis' Occasional Paper and Annual Report of the
Hawaiian Mission (various from 1887); Appeal for the Church in Samoa by the Bishop of
Honolulu (Willis 1897); Lowe to Willis: St Albans 8/2/1901; Willis to Lowe: Honolulu
2/3/1901, 23/3/1901, 28/8/1901 (JBP); ibid. (copy) 18/5/1901 (NAF/DP/DT/3); "Suggested
Diocese of Oceana" (Letter of Lowe to Church Times: St Albans 27/1/1903) pub. 30/1/1903:
133; Lowe to Willis: London 6/6/1900 (referring to appeal to Lord Stanmore) (JBP). 31 Tucker
to Bp. of London: S.P.G., London 16/3/1900 (USPG/CLS/NZ&P/1/495). 32 Willis to Tucker:
Honolulu 3/2/1899 (USPG/CLR/H/242-244); Willis to Lowe: Honolulu (draft) 28/2/1901. 33
Nevill to Abp. of Canterbury: Shelton 1/2/1872 (LPL/186/112); Layreader's Licence of Rev'd
Shirley W. Baker: Dunedin Sept 1900 (JBP); Letter of Willis to Church Times 19/2/1904; Willis
to Lowe: Honolulu 18/5/1901 (JBP). 34 Recognition of Alfred Willis as Missionary Bishop in
Tonga (JBP); Nevill to Abp. of Canterbury: Dunedin (handwritten copy) 3/7/1903 enclosing
'Parnell Resolutions' dated 24/3/1903 (NAF/DP/DT/3). 35 New Zealand Guardian Oct.1902,
Dec.1905, Feb.1907, April 1908, Sept.1910, Oct 1915. 36 Willis to Lowe: Nuku'alofa 14/8/1903
(NAF/DP/DT/3); Nevill to Montgomery: various 1902-1908 (USPG/CLR/NZ&P/3); Bp. of

London to Nevill: London 19/8/1904 (copy) (USPG/CLR/NZ&P/3/232). 37 Letter of Willis to Church Times 19/2/1904; F.T. 15/6/1904, 29/6/1904, 13/7/1904; Polynesian Gazette 25/6/1904. 38 H. Anson to Mrs Willis: St. John's College, Auckland 5/4/1905 (NAF/DP/DT/3); Notes on interview of Mrs Willis by the Rev'd Harold Anson (LPL/FP/Winnigham-Ingram/Willis 1906/148); Montgomery to Mrs Willis: S.P.G., London 14/12/1906 (USPG/CLS/NZ&P/2/107). 39 Pinson 1970: 47- 48; Bp. of London to Montgomery: London 24/10/1906 (USPG/CLR/NZ&P/3/269). 40 Montgomery to Willis: S.P.G., London 27/3/1908 (USPG/CLS/NZ&P/2/147D); Willis to Montgomery: Nuku'alofa 1/10/1908 (USPG/CLR/NZ&P/3/309A). 41 Brandreth 1947: 1-2. 42 Twitchell to Montgomery: Suva 22/2/1909 (USPG/OLR/1910- 1911/50); Willis to Twitchell: Nuku'alofa 24/3/1909, 25/5/1909, 4/4/1910; Willis to Mathews: Nuku'alofa 9/12/1910; Twitchell to Willis: Suva 15/4/1910 (NAF/DP/DT/3). 43 quote from Willis to Nevill: Nuku'alofa 28/3/1911 (USPG/CLR/NZ&P/3/381); Abp. of Canterbury to Twitchell: Lambeth Palace, London 6/7/1909, 8/7/1909, 5/11/1912 (NAF/DP/DT/3). 44 Howard to Twitchell: Tonga College, Nuku'alofa 21/7/1910 (NAF/DP/DT/3). 45 Willis 1915:4. 46 Willis to Montgomery: Nuku'alofa 21/7/1914 (USPG/CLR/NZ&P/4/23); Bp. of Polynesia to Montgomery: Suva 27/8/1915 (USPG/CLR/NZ&P/4/40); Montgomery to Willis: S.P.G., London 20/11/1914 (USPG/CLS/NZ&P/3/50); Montgomery to Twitchell: S.P.G., London 20/11/1914 (USPG/CLS/NZ&P/3/50); Lowe to Pascoe: London 1/11/1912 (USPG/CLR/NZ&P/3/440); Mission Field Jan 1913: 19; F.T. & Herald 8/8/1921; Will of Alfred Willis (Diocesan Office, Suva File TR/2/2/5). 47 Willis to Montgomery: Nuku'alofa 1/10/1908 (USPG/CLR/NZ&P/3/309A); Australasian Methodist Missionary Review 4/2/1909; Forman 1978: 6. 48 Western Pacific Herald 1/10/1909; Scarr 1967: 112; Correspondence with Mission Secretary 10/12/1910 (115/MOMC Mitchell Library) (quoted in Wood 1975: 214); Western Pacific Herald 4/8/1911. 49 Petition of Alfred Willis and others to Sir Francis May; interview of Willis by May; (Western Pacific High Commission File 1911/1152 July 6th); Western Pacific Herald 7/7/1911, 12/7/1911. 50 King George Tupou II to Sir Francis May: Nuku'alofa 7/9/1911 (W.P.H.C.1911/1489) (quoted in Scarr 1967: 114). 51 Willis 1912: 4; Mormonism: Whence is it? The True Story of J. Smith and the Book of Mormon (Willis 1913); letters to writer from Larry Draper: Salt Lake City 27/10/1988 & Helen Moffat: Brigham Young University, Laie 12/10/1988. 52 Willis to Montgomery: Nuku'alofa 3/2/1912 (USPG/CLR/NZ&P/3/395). 53 F.T. 9/5/1912; Hawaiian Church Chronicle Vol.4 No.10 (June 1912): 1, 4, 7, 12; Henry Smith to Willis: Honolulu 8/6/1912 & 18/6/1912 (JBP). 54 Abp. of Canterbury to Twitchell: Lambeth Palace, London 5/11/1912 (NAF/DP/DT/3). 55 Willis to King George Tupou II: Braceborough (handwritten copy) 22/7/1912 (JBP). 56 Otago Witness 8/1/1913; Otago Daily Times 2/1/1913; The Press (Christchurch) 2/1/1913. 57 Otago Daily Times 4/1/1913; St Paul's Cathedral Register of Services & All Saints' Church Vestry Book 5/1/1913 (Hocken Library, Dunedin). 58 The Colonist 16/1/1913, 20/1/1913, 22/1/1913; Nelson Evening Mail 20/1/1913. 59 F.T. 18/2/1913, 20/2/1913.

# CHAPTER 5

# THE END OF THE WILLIS ERA

*"We propose to carry on the work, and if possible extend it, on the lines laid down by our founder" (Strong 1921:2)*

## I

Alfred Willis entered the third decade of the twentieth century with his dream of the Church true and Catholic as the future National Church of Tonga still intact. He was encouraged by moves at an international level to reunite Methodism into its mother Church, and held strongly to the belief that the membership of the Siasi Tau'ataina would join his Anglican Church upon the death of Watkin. Willis' planned endowment of an Eastern Polynesian diocese would assist in making this dream a reality and he encouraged the S.P.G. to appoint an English priest to assist him for the remainder of his life. Willis considered that following his projected retirement in 1923, this man should be raised to the episcopate.[1]

Despite the interruption caused by the mahaki faka'auha, Willis was making progress on his `corrected' translation of the Bible in Tongan. He considered that this work would be his lasting contribution to Tongan Christianity, and saw the completion of the project as being of high priority. As was his habit, Willis had kept up a steady stream of polemical pamphlets, letters and articles, and had published, in 1916, the first of three volumes of his rebuttal of higher criticism of the Bible entitled *The Unity of the Bible*.[2]

St. Andrew's School, after a shaky beginning, had shown a steady growth in roll, and Willis was encouraged by the confirmation of six St. Andrew's boys on 1st December 1919. Willis hoped that they would be amongst the future leaders of the Church. Nelson Tu'itavake, one of those confirmed, travelled to Auckland in early 1920 to join other ex-students of St. Andrew's School sent by Willis to advance their studies at St. Stephen's School in Parnell, Auckland.[3]

The construction of a `permanent' church building, long dear to Willis' heart, had seen a little progress in the previous few years. Willis had long believed that as a judge could only dispense justice in the courthouse, the Anglican clergyman, in like fashion, required a suitable edifice in which to administer the Christian religion. The flimsy wooden buildings which Willis had been forced to erect due to the shortage of funds, were to Willis, never more than temporary places of worship.[4] In response to a reference to this 'permanent' church in Willis' *Letter for 1914*, Dr. C.G. Campbell, who had supported his grandiose ambitions since their visits of 1902 and 1903, promised 'substantial aid' for the construction of the future cathedral of an Eastern Polynesian diocese. Campbell suggested the adaptation of a traditional Tongan fale in a cruciform shape. He considered that whatever was built would be the model for future church buildings in Tonga. Willis was not convinced of the 'correctness' of this adapted Tongan style and gave the London architect engaged on his behalf by the Church Crafts League, specifications that were textbook Ecclesialogical Society. These included a spacious sanctuary, a chancel with stalls, and a rood screen.[5]

With some small donations, Willis established a Nuku'alofa Church Building Fund. Anticipating raising the finance amongst his English supporters, as he had done for the construction of St. Andrew's Cathedral in Honolulu, he accepted the fact that it would be several years before this project could be realised due to the continuation of the war in Europe.

Upon the death of his sister Henrietta Wainwright in 1915, Willis had received a bequest for the work of the Church in Tonga. This he had invested through the S.P.G., the interest being used to supplement the stipend of Sang Mark.[6]

Such was the inflated view of the Anglican Church in Tonga which Willis presented to himself and to the outside world. He ignored the reality of a total active Church membership, Tongan and palangi, of less than two hundred in the Kingdom, scattered across over one hundred and fifty miles of ocean, and weakened by lack of regular ministry, defections and the mahaki faka'auha. Despite the Wainwright bequest, financial contributions had decreased from both local and overseas sources, and the prospect of supporting other staff aside from the faithful Sang Mark, looked bleak.

Willis' health had declined due to the passage of time and the exertion of burying the dead and caring for the living during the mahaki faka'auha.[7] Although Willis was prepared to retire in favour of a younger man by 1923, by which time he would be eighty seven years old, Willis had made no effort to delegate authority to Sang Mark. Despite his recognition of his assistant priest's abilities, Willis had listened for too long to the bigoted remarks of certain Australasian members of the palangi community, and was convinced that a Chinese could never head the Anglican Church in Tonga. Consequently, the one person who most fully shared his vision for the

Anglican Church in the Kingdom was likely to be passed over. Since Filipe Vea's death in 1913, Willis had made no effort to encourage an ordained native ministry, and by 1920, only the southern islands of Vava'u had Tongan layreaders for their congregations. Whilst a success in itself, St. Andrew's School had drained the island congregations of young people. Those who continued on to St. Stephen's School in Auckland were even further removed from the congregations that desperately required their youthful involvement.

Alfred Willis left Nuku'alofa in April 1920 in order to travel to London to the Lambeth Conference and Pan Anglican Congress due to begin in July of that year. He looked forward to being reunited with Mrs Willis after four years of separation. He also hoped to complete his 'corrected' translation of the Bible and arrange publication of this work and the two remaining volumes of *The Unity of the Bible*. It was his intention that he and Mrs Willis would return to Tonga before Christmas 1920.[8]

Willis had not attempted to attend the 1908 Lambeth Conference, as the problems with the Bishop of London and the English authorities surrounding his work in Tonga at that time were not completely resolved. Now he was able to take his rightful place as a bishop of the Anglican Church, and in addition, hear tribute from a fellow bishop from the most unlikely quarter, that of the Protestant Episcopal Church. This 'saintly apostle of the Pacific' *(Partridge to Pascoe: Westminster 19/7/1920 USPG/ CLR/ NZ&P/ 4/97)* was also encouraged in his work in reuniting the religiously disaffected, by further positive discussion at the Conference of reunion with the Methodists.[9]

Following what Willis considered to be this most successful event, he met with C. Cogswell, his architect, to discuss plans for the 'permanent' church. Despite the small amount in the building fund, Willis wanted sketch plans to take back with him to Tonga. He booked passages on the *Athenic* for Mrs Willis and himself to sail for New Zealand in January 1921, and they retired in early October to the quiet Hampshire town of Milford-on-Sea to complete his Bible project. Unaccustomed to the cool and damp of an English autumn, Willis caught a chill, and after a short illness, died of pneumonia on Sunday 14th November 1920. He was buried in the local churchyard.[10] Thus ended the earthly career of this 'fossil of the nineteenth century', as Willis had once described himself to the Bishop of London.[11] He outlived most of his contemporaries and held to his death a view of the Church which was rooted in a period some fifty years earlier.

The originator of the vision of the Church true and Catholic as the National Church of Tonga may have died, but there were still those who were more or less committed to working for its fulfilment.

The Rev'd Yim Sang Mark had run the Church single handed following Willis' departure, ministering to the European congregation in Kolofo'ou, in addition to his normal work at the school and with the Tongan congregations. The year 1920 had actually seen some progress amongst the European community; the Sunday school, in recess since 1915, had been reopened and was flourishing. Despite Willis' fears, Sang Mark was popular with most of the palangi community.

Sang Mark and 'Ana, along with the members of Willis' Church, were most distressed by their elderly patriarch's death. However they anticipated that little would change, the late bishop's family and friends supporting the work of the Church as they had always done, and that Willis' vision for the Church would eventually be realised.[12]

Meanwhile in England, both the S.P.G. and the hapless Bishop Twitchell were acting independently on Willis' desire for an English priest to head the Anglican Church in Tonga. Within two weeks, the Rev'd William Barnes, a former S.P.G. office staff member, volunteered to go out to Tonga to "carry on during the emergency" *( Pascoe to Twitchell: S.P.G. 2/12/1920 USPG/ CLS/ NZ&P/ 3/123)*. Barnes had been Willis' curate at the Cathedral in Honolulu during the Second Congregation fiasco of the mid 1880s, and had left for Canada in disgust at his bishop's antics in 1892.[13] Presumably with the elderly autocrat safely out of the way, he was willing again to risk being involved again in one of his missionary endeavours.

But Twitchell pre-empted efforts by the Society to find a priest to move to Tonga. Despite his complete lack of knowledge or involvement in Willis' Anglican Church, apart from a single short visit in 1909, he confidently appointed the Rev'd Edward H. Strong, describing him as "a keen missionary and a lover of the South Seas" *(USPG/ OLR/ A,NZ&P/ 1918-1921 /62 )*.

Strong, a New Zealander, was an unlikely choice, having spent most of his career teaching in theological institutions in both New Zealand and England. He had most recently resigned as vice-principal of Willis' former theological college at Wells. He had taken no earlier interest in Willis' work in Tonga, his missionary interests having been with the Melanesian Mission. Strong returned to New Zealand, and in February 1921 telegraphed to Twitchell his acceptance of the appointment to Tonga, agreeing to the offered annual stipend of three hundred pounds. He also requested that Twitchell insert in *Crockford's Clerical Directory* that he had commenced his Tongan appointment in 1920![14]

Strong arrived unannounced in Tonga on the steamer *Tofua* in early May 1921, Twitchell having neglected to inform Sang Mark of Strong's appointment, or to provide the new head of the Tongan Mission with a licence. Strong found the Church in good health, and was appreciative of Sang Mark's efforts in maintaining Willis' work. However, Sang Mark had been reduced to penury, having received no financial support from overseas since Willis' death in November 1920. Willis had drawn all of his S.P.G. grant for 1920 but this, along with the rest of Willis' finances, including his drawings from the Tongan Mission Fund, had been frozen upon his death. Sang Mark had run the school and the Church on the tiny local contributions and what he could earn from the school workshop, going into considerable debt with local trading firms. Strong guaranteed Sang Mark's debts, and due to his own misunderstanding of the S.P.G. grant system, Strong did not receive any stipend for several months.[15]

Strong was initially enthusiastic for the work in Tonga, and suggested that a memorial fund be set up to train Tongan ordination candidates. He considered that there were at least three boys showed some sign of vocation, including Paula Vea (son of Lesieli and the late Filipe), Siosaia Onetaka from Ovaka, and Kesomi Pota Langi (a nephew of 'Ana Mark). He believed they should be sent to St. Stephen's School for further education. Strong also initiated a project for an Anglican Church school for Europeans and part-Europeans. Within two months of his arrival Strong had circulated the palangi community, and put together a board under his chairmanship, along with the acting Premier, Tungī Mailefihi (as Minister of Education), Sang Mark, and a number of leading European residents including Mrs Dawson, Mr Darrell- Wall (the auditor-general), Ragnor Hyne (Director of Education) and A.H. Gould (manager of Burns Philp Ltd).[16] Strong styled his proposed school St. Aidan's and appealed to the S.P.G. for funds and "a couple of sisters from some English community... if they are sensible women and not faddists."*( Strong to Bp. King: Nuku'alofa 24/6/1921 USPG/CLR/NZ&P/4/110E)* Strong considered that the tropics was not a suitable place for young single women teachers of the kind he could obtain from New Zealand or Australian teacher training colleges!

Strong soon became disillusioned with the Church which Willis had established in Tonga. Although initially he blamed the Bishop of Polynesia for his problems, especially those of finance, he soon began to realise the impracticality of Willis' Church true and Catholic in Tonga.

He came to the conclusion that Willis had been badly mistaken in coming to Tonga at all, and that there was no work in the Kingdom for the Anglican Church except amongst the `white population' who he believed would be best served by an itinerant priest. He dismissed the belief which was strongly held by Sang Mark, and encouraged by the Premier, Polutele Tu'ivakanö, that the Tau'ataina would all become Anglicans upon the death of Watkin.[17]

Unfortunately Edward Strong combined this ability to see the Tongan Anglican Mission in a wider perspective with a negative disposition and a sharp cutting tongue. This did not help Sang Mark to see the impossibility of fulfilling Willis' vision. He was deeply hurt by both Strong's criticism of his deceased patron, and his suggestion that he should leave Tonga and work amongst his own Chinese people. Twitchell resigned his see in September 1921, leaving Sang Mark no higher authority to whom he could appeal. He had no choice but to accept Strong's authority as head of the Mission. Sang Mark continued his work amongst the Tongan congregations, the school and workshop as he had done before Strong's arrival. The head of the Mission worked only with the palangi membership and did not leave Nuku'alofa in the ten months he was resident in the Kingdom.[18]

Edward Strong resigned as head of the Tongan Anglican Mission and Archdeacon of Tonga in March 1922, having sent more letters to the S.P.G. in ten months than Willis had in the previous ten years. R.T. Mathews, the vicar of Suva, as administrator of the diocese (who described himself as the `Pooh Bah of Polynesia'), attempted to make an internal appointment from amongst the tiny diocesan staff. The Rev'd G. Forrest-Sale, the vicar of Levuka, initially offered to go to Tonga, desiring some respite from the oppressive humidity and numerous Asiatics of the old Fijian capital. After taking advice, possibly from Strong, who passed through Levuka en route to New Zealand, Forrest-Sale changed his mind, although as late as December 1922 he was still reconsidering the position.[19] When this failed, Sang Mark was left, by default, to run the Anglican Church in Tonga as best he could on the two hundred pound grant originally intended as a supplement to Willis' private income. The short stay and tactless approach of Strong had strengthened Sang Mark's resolve to remain in Tonga and attempt to bring to fruition the hopes of Willis that the Anglican Church would yet play a leading role in Tonga's religious affairs.

When Lionel Kempthorne, a New Zealander, was appointed the second Bishop in Polynesia in 1923, initially little changed in the work of what was now consistently referred to as the Tongan Mission. He was impressed with the character and abilities of Sang Mark in attempting to continue the work virtually single handed and under the constraints of lack of finance and some racial prejudice. Sang Mark, for his part, was pleased to have the moral and administrative support of a bishop, albeit in Suva, who could make, at the very least, annual trips to Tonga to conduct confirmations.

To assist Sang Mark in his work, Kempthorne convinced John and Tom Dodd, who had been running a small private school in Suva for some time, to move to Tonga in early 1924. They established a school for European and part-European children, with the addition of the senior class from St. Andrew's School, at Willis' former residence. Kempthorne licensed John Dodd, who had attended St. Aidan's Theological College in Birkenhead, Lancashire, for two years, as a layreader with responsibility for the European congregation. The Bishop also considered the possibility of ordaining him at some future date.[20]

In the same year that the Dodd brothers arrived, the Kingdom was disrupted by the attempt to reunite the two branches of lotu Uesiliana. The involvement of firstly Sang Mark, and later John Dodd, in the controversies stemmed primarily from Willis' belief that the Anglican Church needed to be ready to receive the membership of the Siasi Tau'ataina into their ranks upon their inevitable disintegration. Sang Mark appeared as a witness in the Land Court case which the break away section of the old Siasi Tau'ataina, led by Watkin and Finau 'Ulukalala, brought against the newly reunited Free Wesleyan Church of Tonga (or Siasi Uesiliana Tau'ataina 'o Tonga). The Tau'ataina claimed that they were the true successors of the Church of King George Tupou I and the new Siasi Uesiliana had no right to take over the land leases and other assets of the old Siasi Tau'ataina. Sang Mark repeated many of Watkin's criticisms of the Moulton translation of the Bible in his testimony in an effort to prove this fact. The Watkin-'Ulukalala party, who styled their Church Siasi Tau'ataina 'o Tonga, initially won the case, although it was overturned on appeal to the Privy Council later in the year. [21]

Sang Mark was probably encouraged in his support of Watkin by the `beach' community, who were considered to have been protagonists in the whole affair for their own political ends. Many of these people were, nominally at least, Anglicans, including Watkin's son-in-law, J.E. Masterton who had been acting British Agent and Consul for much of 1924. They had made quiet stirrings within Tonga, and also provided inaccurate and inflated reports in the foreign press concerning events in Tonga, giving the picture of a persecuted minority of true Wesleyans fighting for their survival, parallels having been drawn with the Scottish Wee Free movement of the early twentieth century. In addition to his appearance in the court case, Sang Mark was also persuaded to print polemical material on the Anglican Church press for the Siasi Tau'ataina, this work occupying many evenings for Sang Mark and 'Ana's nephew 'Asita over several months.[22]

The Rev'd Jabez Watkin, forty years head of the Siasi Tau'ataina, old and new, died in January 1925. After a short period when Uatasoni Kolo was acting president, the Siasi Tau'ataina chose John Dodd, Anglican layreader and schoolteacher, as their new president.

Dodd's presidency was certainly seen by the Siasi Uesiliana as another Anglican attempt to woo the Siasi Tau'ataina, the palangi Wesleyan missionaries having long resented Anglican work amongst the Tongan population. Although this was possibly the case, there were definitely other factors involved. There was continuing palangi sympathy for the Siasi Tau'ataina cause, the Queen Victoria Memorial Hall having been made available for worship and a school. The reported salary of six hundred pounds, with three hundred pounds for his brother Tom as principal of the school run by the Siasi Tau'ataina, and the kudos involved in being head of a much larger body than the Anglicans, were certainly attractions. In addition, in accepting the post it afforded an opportunity to gain some ascendancy over Sang Mark, whom Dodd disliked.[23]

John Dodd's glorious days as president of the Siasi Tau'ataina 'o Tonga were short lived. He returned from an extended visitation to the islands of Ha'apai and Vava'u in the company of the young Fine Halapua and Tevita Taumoepeau, a Tau'ataina student at Dodd's school, to find Sang Mark returned from the 1925 synod in Suva, in the company of Bishop Kempthorne.

Kempthorne was annoyed and embarrassed at what he considered to gross interference by Anglicans in the affairs of other denominations. For the second time in less than a year he had been required to smooth over trouble caused by his staff, having visited Queen Salote the previous November following Sang Mark's involvement in the Land Court case. John Dodd resigned in preference to severing all connection with the Anglican Church, realising that when he inevitably moved on, the status he held in Tonga would mean very little to those outside the Kingdom.[24] No mass movement to the Anglican Church resulted from Dodd's resignation from the presidency of the Siasi Tau'ataina.

The nett result for the Tongan Mission of these two disrupted years was twofold. Firstly, the myth of the long hoped-for mass swelling of the ranks of the Anglican Church by the Tau'ataina was finally exploded. Even had Polutele Tu'ivakanō been still alive, it would have been unlikely than more than a handful would have followed him to the Church true and Catholic from where he had launched his political come back some twenty years before. The practice and outlook of the Anglican Church had moved a long way from the period of Shirley Baker and the early years of Alfred Willis, and would have been as foreign as Roman Catholicism to the bulk of the Tau'ataina members.

Secondly, Kempthorne had visited the London headquarters of the S.P.G. before his consecration and he had been much more influenced by the correspondence resulting form Edward Strong's ten month sojourn in Tonga than the grandiose schemes of Alfred Willis. The events of 1924 and 1925 had endorsed Strong's opinions and strengthened Kempthorne's resolve to guide the Church to better ways in Tonga.[25]

During his 1924 visit, Kempthorne had established a Church Committee in Nuku'alofa, which consisted largely of Europeans, with, ironically, John Dodd as its secretary, a position he held until his departure in 1928. This committee, in consultation with the Bishop and Standing Committee in Suva, controlled the funds of the Mission, which were still almost entirely derived from S.P.G. grants and some interest from the Wainwright bequest and Willis' diocesan endowment.[26]

Whilst Sang Mark had lost some control over local affairs, greater involvement of the bishop in the Tongan Mission had some benefits. Kempthorne took over responsibility for the training of Tongans for future ordained ministry. His first move in this area was to arrange for Nelson Tu'itavake, on his return from St. Stephen's School in mid 1925, to continue his studies whilst working as a pupil teacher at St. Andrew's School. He arranged for a place for Tu'itavake to be available at St. John's College, Auckland in 1927 if he came up to sufficient standard and providing his family could come up with the necessary money for the fees. In the same year, Kempthorne arranged for Paula Vea to enter St. Stephen's School with the hope that he too should go on to St. John's College. Financial assistance was given by the New Zealand Anglican Board of Missions.[27]

Tu'itavake was dismissed from St. Andrew's School in 1928 and did not continue his studies for the ordained ministry. Paula Vea returned from St. Stephen's School in 1929 and assisted at St. Andrew's School and as a layreader at St. Paul's Church. He had some success in his theological exams taken by correspondence, but never entered St. John's College. He was never ordained and died in 1942 aged only thirty six.

Kempthorne made the same error as Willis had before him, in that he saw the only route to the priesthood being through the English model of grammar school and theological college, a process which generally put Tongans at a disadvantage due to their poorer English. Whilst this was probably the earliest attempt to train local ordained ministers in the Diocese of Polynesia, Kempthorne failed to understand that learning could take place with satisfactory results in languages other than English. The Siasi Fakaongo had trained their ministers to a high standard in the vernacular for over sixty years at Tupou College, and numerous other examples had existed in the South Pacific for several decades.[28]

Paula Vea was the last Tongan Anglican to be sent to St. Stephen's School in this period. As those whom initially Willis, and later Sang Mark, had encouraged trickled back into the Kingdom, it became clear that the education which they received was of little benefit to the Church in Nuku'alofa or the island congregations. Most of those who went to New Zealand did so in their late teens, and entered primary classes with Maori boys who were several years their junior. They had found the experience humiliating and although they were living with fellow Polynesians, the different expectations and mores learned during their school days in New Zealand did not allow them to fit easily into their own land and culture on their return. In addition, those from the islands now preferred the relative sophistication of Nuku'alofa to returning to their isolated villages.

## II

The year 1925 was a watershed for the Anglican Church which Willis has established in Tonga. Willis had inherited the island congregations from Baker's Church, and he put so much effort in developing them as centres for the future expansion of the Anglican Church in the Kingdom. Following many years of decline, after 1925 they ceased to be of any real significance to the work of the Tongan Anglican Mission.

Since Willis' departure for England in April 1920, simple maintenance of these congregations had become an increasingly difficult task. Sang Mark's

heavy responsibilities in the school and Church, and the necessity of earning extra money from his workshop activities, had restricted the time available for travelling, leaving only the twice-annual school holidays free for this task. This had become the pattern for the 1920s and Strong's short sojourn and the appointment of a new bishop in Suva had made little difference. The restricted timetable of the Union Steam Ship Company mail steamers initially operated as a wartime measure, was continued in the depressed economic conditions in the South Pacific in the 1920s. Sang Mark was often forced to travel by whatever means was available, from tramp steamers and cutters, to small open boasts. He was a terrible sailor, writing in later life;
"I found it best to eat... ripe bananas so as to have something to  evacuate when necessary. I always found a nice spot on the ship so I could feed the fishes." (Mark 1964:3) Sang Mark also was involved in a number of shipwrecks, the most notable being the foundering of the Norwegian steamer Mesner on Hakaufisi near Nomuka, Ha'apai in September 1924.   Such problems further complicated his near impossible task.

Whenever possible, Sang Mark took some of his St. Andrew's School students during these school holiday visits. This was primarily to assist in maintaining the buildings of the Church which was increasingly difficult for the ageing and dwindling congregations. He hoped that their presence would encourage the local Anglicans isolated from the more vigorous Church life in Nuku'alofa.[29]

It was initially in Ha'apai that the lack of regular ministry took its toll on the tiny weak congregations. Mo'unga-one had always been a difficult place to regularly service, and was drastically weakened in both leadership and membership by the mahaki faka'auha of 1918. This was the first congregation to die completely, no services being held at Mo'unga-one after 1924. The Church of St. Philip and St. James, stripped of its ecclesiastical accoutrements, remained standing for many years until finally flattened in a hurricane.[30] In Lifuka, numbers in both the Tongan and English speaking congregations were tiny at the beginning of the decade. Tongan work soon fell away to almost nothing. Sang Mark and Bishop Kempthorne kept up an itinerant ministry to the handful of European Anglicans. Included in their number were the two remaining daughters of Shirley Baker who continued to run their school at Fakapale.[31]

The erratic exercise of the priestly ministry was a major factor in the decline of the Anglican Church in the southern islands of Vava'u in the 1920s. But the single most important event was the death of Siliveinusi

Lavulavu in late 1921 at the age of sixty nine. He had ruled over the Anglican Church, and Lape, for over twenty years, and certainly within the Church little alternative leadership had grown up to rival his claim. Melieli Kite had continued his work as a layreader after Lavulavu's death, but without the traditional power base or education that had been the key to Lavulavu's success. Kite was not a young man, and he found it difficult to keep up the work of the Church consistently in the weaker centres of Ovaka and Nuapapu. These two villages, where the Anglicans were in the minority, exhibited many features in common with Ha'apai, including older congregations, weak leadership and families with divided denominational loyalties. Willis had attempted to strengthen the Ovaka congregation by appointing Siosaia Fifita Lavulavu, a matapule who had been an Anglican since 1903, as layreader in 1918. But his frequent absences in Neiafu did not provide the consistent leadership that was necessary.[32]

The southern islands of Vava'u had provided proportionally more students for St. Andrew's School than any other area outside of Kolofo'ou, but the extended absences of the youthful component vital for healthy Church life contributed to further weaken the Church. Lavulavu's own family, to whom it would be expected that leadership roles would be likely to fall, became scattered throughout Vava'u and Tonga, and his son Saimone Laulile did not return from New Zealand for several years after finishing at St. Stephen's School. Willis' policy of centralising his education system, whilst being more efficient of teaching staff and other scarce resources, in the long run caused more harm than good to these island congregations.

Kempthorne visited Lape in late 1923 and conducted a confirmation for five young adults, being most impressed with the response of the Anglican Church membership to his presence. His return to the area in 1926, when he confirmed one person at Ovaka, did not produce the same effect. The death of Melieli Kite at Lape the previous year had coincided with the continuing religious disturbances that beset the Kingdom. Devoid of effective leadership, most Anglicans joined one or other of the rival forms of lotu Uesiliana. A scattered handful of faithful Anglicans remained at Ovaka, providing a core for later Anglican expansion in Neiafu in the 1950s. Sang Mark continued to visit the area until his departure for Honolulu in 1928, but the days of Alfred Willis' most successful island mission were over.[33] The prophecy of Siliveinusi Lavulavu that the Anglican Church in these southern islands of Vava'u would not survive long after his death was fulfilled.

By 1925, the prospect of realising the ambition of Willis for a 'permanent' church building in Nuku'alofa appeared closer. On his death, the small building fund which Willis had established, passed to his brother-in-law, H.B. Simeon and William Lowe as executors of his estate. They, with other members of Willis' now aged family and some of his former Iolani College students living in London, formed a memorial committee which canvassed for funds to build the church in his memory. They had been somewhat dismayed by Strong's rival appeal for funds for the training of Tongan ordination candidates, but had reluctantly altered their aims to include Strong's project. After Strong's departure, they quietly ignored the alternative object and concentrated their efforts on the building project that was much nearer to their hearts.[34]

This committee secured the residue of the Tongan Mission Fund which Willis' youngest sister Louisa had run from their Braceborough home, and any further contributions went to the memorial fund rather than on-going support for the Mission. In addition, they attempted unsuccessfully to divert the capital sum of the Wainwright bequest to their project. Bishop H.H. Montgomery had warned of the danger of special missionary funds for the support of an individual bishop in a pamphlet which he had written in 1903, concerned at what may happen on the death or translation of the object of their fundraising. Both Willis' move to Tonga, which had taken support from the Hawaiian Church, and these events following his death, certainly bore out his opinions.[35]

Beside the Nuku'alofa Church Building Fund, Willis had bequeathed any property leases held in his name in the Kingdom to the Anglican Church in Tonga. His remaining property and investments in Hawai'i were sold to endow the future Eastern Polynesian diocese. The conditions on both these bequests were such, however, that they were not available to the memorial committee. In fact, those on the endowment were so strict and complex that they could not be met, and although the income generated was made available for the use of the Tongan Mission, the capital sum was never handed to any other body by the S.P.G. because Willis' hoped- for diocese never eventuated. Under the terms of the bequest, the capital sum of around two thousand pounds was to pass to the New Zealand Church if no such diocese was formed, but they also were unable to fulfil the complex conditions. Lengthy and expensive negotiations with the Charity Commissioners in London in the 1930s consumed much of the capital[36]

Kempthorne had met with William Lowe when in London in 1923 and was keen for the building project to proceed. With some chance of a more peaceful religious atmosphere in the Kingdom, and over five hundred pounds in the bank in London, with the promise of another one thousand pounds to come on the death of Eliza, one of Willis' younger sisters, the memorial committee were ready to make more definite plans.

Sang Mark visited Honolulu following the 1926 synod in Suva and launched an appeal amongst the former students of Iolani College. By early 1927 he was urging the adoption of a modified plan which would improve ventilation and decrease costs. Sang Mark was keen to begin construction immediately under his supervision. However this proposal, as with all made from Tonga, was met with objections from the architect in London, with whom the ageing and increasingly forgetful William Lowe was the main contact. Lowe insisted on circulating any plans or alterations amongst the few remaining members of Willis' family who were interested in the project, creating long delays and many misunderstandings between Kempthorne, Lowe and the building committee in Nuku'alofa which consisted of Sang Mark, J. Darrell-Wall, John Dodd, W.S. White, F. Riechelmann, Malakai Tukuafu and Sulio Taufa.[37]

In the midst of negotiations for the long awaited construction of this memorial to Alfred Willis, Sang Mark announced that he had, in December 1927, received a request from the Bishop of Hawai'i to take up the post of rector of St. Peter's Chinese Church in Honolulu. His acceptance sent shockwaves as far as William Lowe's comfortable smoking room in St. Albans, dismayed that Sang Mark would not be available to oversee the building of the church.[38]

Sang Mark's decision to accept the post was hardly surprising. The period since his elderly mentor's death had been one of financial hardship and disappointment, as he had seen much of what he and Willis had laboured so hard to establish wasted away. His visit to his dying father in Honolulu in 1926 had unsettled and disillusioned him immensely, and on his return to Tonga, the physical and cultural isolation of the Kingdom had become apparent to him. Sang Mark had initiated Anglican work among the Chinese community in Suva during the 1925 synod, when he had baptised ten children, his action having led to a request from the Chinese of that city for their own missioner. However Sang Mark considered it unlikely that he would ever be able to work full time again amongst his own people, because of the lack of proficiency in the Hakka dialect. The invitation from Honolulu therefore had been a surprise, and he gladly agreed to go and build up a congregation, that despite internal problems over recent years, had the promise of financial and moral support that was lacking in Tonga.[39]

Kempthorne was also reluctant to lose Sang Mark's abilities as a building supervisor, but after correspondence with Bishop J. La Mothe in Honolulu, agreed to release Sang Mark in August 1928. His remaining few months in the Kingdom were spent with the children of St. Andrew's School and the Kolofo'ou congregation collecting rocks from the nearby reef to be broken up for concrete for the new church, using a launch and punt that had been purchased with funds from Suva. Further problems with the receipt of plans postponed the commencement of construction.[40]

Sang Mark and 'Ana's departure severed yet another link with the Church of Alfred Willis. 'Ana Tautala Kilakepa Langi had been a student in Baker's Kolisi Fefine in Kolofo'ou and had been Mrs Willis' maid from soon after Sang Mark's arrival in August 1902 until their marriage in February 1911. She had assisted Willis and Sang Mark with their translations of services and hymns. She, like Sang Mark, had worked long hours in the Church for little pay, taking on a multitude of responsibilities including, in later years, teaching at St. Andrew's School and running a girls' hostel known as St. Mary's at their Pahu 'api. Sang Mark's close association with Willis from the age of twelve had left him with a particular view of the Church true and Catholic close to that of his patron, but untainted by the dogmatism that often neutralised Willis' good points. His easy manner with his wife's relations and their neighbours in Pahu, won him a number of converts for the Anglican Church, particularly during the 1920s.[41]

The Marks left the Kolofo'ou congregation in a healthier state than it had been at the beginning of the decade, with growing numbers and a number of strong leaders and potential leaders. St. Andrew's School was, if anything, over popular, with 'Ana teaching a class of over sixty, assisted only by her nephew Kesomi Pota Langi. The roll had increased markedly with the Dodd brothers departure for New Zealand in May 1928. St. Andrew's School had developed a respected place amongst the schools of the Kingdom under Sang Mark's leadership and he had provided valuable training in the practical work skills of carpentry, cartwrighting, printing and mechanics.[42]

Kempthorne installed the Rev'd E.R. Elder from Australia to temporarily replace Sang Mark. Whilst in Tonga, he arranged for a local building contractor to construct the new church. Elder was replaced in January 1929 by the Rev'd Harold Favell, to whom fell the task of seeing this project to its completion.

The church was completed in mid 1930. The entire sum of two thousand seven hundred pounds for its construction had come from outside the Kingdom, the largest portion being the residues of the estates of Willis' three younger unmarried sisters, Augusta, Eliza and Louisa. The Tongan and European congregations provided the furniture and internal fittings. Apart from a few minor modifications, it had been built to the specifications given by Willis to his architect in 1915.[43]

This building on the Church 'api which it shared with St. Andrew's School, enshrined in concrete the Catholic doctrine of Alfred Willis, in which the Kolofo'ou congregation worshipped using his Tongan Prayer Book. This was virtually all that now remained of the grand scheme of the Right Reverend Alfred Willis D.D. to make the Anglican Church the National Church of Tonga. The consecration of the Willis Memorial Church of St. Paul on Ascension Day 1931, despite a debt of one hundred and fifty pounds which Kempthorne personally guaranteed, effectively marked the end of the Willis era.[44]

# CHAPTER FIVE - SOURCE NOTES

1 Willis to Montgomery: Nuku'alofa 30/6/1919 (USPG/CLR/NZ&P/4/92). 2 Willis 1917; Willis 1919:4. 3 Mission Field Sept.1921: 156; ACR: 112; Sermon notes (in Tongan) in Willis' handwriting for 1/12/1919 (JBP); St.. Stephen's School Attendance Records - Quarterly Returns 1913- 1942 (NANZ.BAAA/1001/25c. 4 Sermon text of Alfred Willis printed in Polynesian Gazette 25/6/1904; 'Temporary Church of St. Peter and St. Paul' (ACR). 5 Campbell to Willis: New York 27/6/1915, 15/10/1915, 22/6/1916; Cogswell to Willis: London 15/10/1915; Willis to Cogswell: Nuku'alofa 29/1/1916 (NAF/DP/DT/11). 6 Anglican Church Accounts for 1918. 7 Interview with Latai Havili: Kolomotu'a 31/8/1988. 8 F.T. & Herald 19/4/1920; Willis to Bp. King: Milford on Sea 22/10/1920 (USPG/CLR/NZ&P/4/99). 9 Bp. Sidney Partridge to Pascoe: Westminster 19/7/1920 (USPG/CLR/NZ&P/4/97). 10 Lowe to Pascoe: St. Albans 14/6/1921 (USPG/CLR/NZ&P/4/106); C. Mathews to Sec. of S.P.G.: Lymington 14/11/1920 (USPG/OLR/NZ&P/66). 11 Willis to Twitchell: Nuku'alofa 24/9/1909 quoting letter written to Bp. of London: 22/1/1907 (NAF/DP/DT/4). 12 Mission Field Sept.1921: 156; Y.S. Mark to Mrs Willis: Nuku'alofa 11/4/1922 (NAF/DP/DT/5). 13 Pascoe to Twitchell: S.P.G., London (USPG/CLS/NZ&P/3/123); Barnes to Tucker: Honolulu 19/2/1892 (USPG/CLR/H/1871-1910/171). 14 S.P.G. Application for the appointment of an missionary (USPG/OLR/A,NZ&P/1918-1921/62); Wells Theological College- Presentor's Book, Michaelmas Term 1920 (Wells Record Office/2308/WTC/R/7); Twitchell to Bp. King: Hull 21/2/1921. 15 Strong to Bp. King: Nuku'alofa 24/6/1921 (USPG/CLR/NZ&P/4/104); ibid.2/9/1921 (USPG/CLR/NZ&P/4/115C); Strong to Garnett: Nuku'alofa 24/2/1922 (USPG/CLR/NZ&P/4/131); Mark 1960. 16 Strong 1921: 2. 17 Strong to Bp. King: Nuku'alofa 2/9/1921 (USPG/CLR/NZ&P/4/115C). 18 Interview with Ileoraine Pegler: Kolofo'ou 18/11/1988; Sullivan 1975: 55; Lowe to Sec. of S.P.G.: London 10/1/1922 enclosing Y.S. Mark to Lowe: Nuku'alofa 26/11/1921 (USPG/CLR/NZ&P/4/126); Y.S. Mark to Mrs Willis: Nuku'alofa 11/4/1922 (NAF/DP/DT/5); Mark 1960. 19 Mathews to Sec. of S.P.G.: Suva 3/9/1922 (USPG/CLR/NZ&P/4/151A); Forrest-Sale to Dolphin: Levuka 22/3/1922 (USPG/CLR/NZ&P/4/141); Mathews to Bp. King: Suva 19/6/1922 (USPG/CLR/NZ&P/4/142); Forrest-Sale to Mathews: Levuka 6/12/1922, 8/12/1922 (USPG/CLR/NZ&P/4/158). 20 Kempthorne to Bp. King: Suva 14/12/1923 (USPG/OLR/NZ&P/281/85); F.T. & Herald 16/4/1925; interview with Bp. Fine Halapua: Halaleva 28/4/1988; R.J. Howard to Kempthorne: Birkenhead 8/7/1924 (NAF/DP/HO III/Correspondence J. Dodd 1924-1929). 21 Ellem 1983: 163-182; Forman 1974: 3- 21; letter of Dr. A.H. Wood to writer: Mont Albert, Vic. 18/9/1987; Tongan Law Reports Vol.II 1963: 8-9, 136. 22 Ellem 1983: 171; ACR; Wood 1926: 6; Pacific Press 29/9/1924; interview with Asita Langi: Mangaia 20/9/1988. 23 Page to McCallum: Nuku'alofa 29/6/1925 (Free Wesleyan Church Archives, Nuku'alofa)(quoted in Wood 1975: 227); Strong to Bp. King: Nuku'alofa 31/1/1922 (USPG/CLR/NZ&P/4/143); F.T. & Herald 5/8/1925, 16/4/1925. 24 Interview with Bp. Fine Halapua: Halaleva 28/4/1988; interview with Asita Langi: Mangaia 20/9/1988; A.B.M. Review 12/9/1925: 111. No correspondence of this period with the protagonists survived in the Diocese of Polynesia records. 25 Dolphin to Y.S.Mark: S.P.G., London 6/2/1923 (USPG/CLS/NZ&P/3/179); Strong to Sec. of

110

S.P.G.: Nuku'alofa 13/3/1922 (USPG/CLR/NZ&P/4/140); ibid. 31/3/1922, ibid.: New Plymouth 24/6/1922 (USPG/CLR/NZ&P/4/143). 26 Y.S. Mark to Archd. Hands: Nuku'alofa 1/5/1928 (NAF/DP/DT/5); Polynesia Form 2A - Statistics to 31/12/1924 (USPG/MR/1924/1/56); USPG/Ledger - Foreign Diocese: 484. 27 A.B.M. Review 12/9/1925: 111; Tisdall to Kempthorne: St. John's College, Auckland 26/10/1927 (NAF/DP/HO III/Correspondence N. Tu'itavake (1926-1927); Albert Wilson to Kempthorne: St. Stephen's School, Parnell 17/7/1925, 22/12/1925 (NAF/DP/HO III/Correspondence B. Vea 1925-1940). 28 Annual Inspection for 1921 (St. Stephen's School Correspondence 1905-1922 NANZ/BAAA/1001/1029B); Baula Vea to Kempthorne: St. Stephen's School, Parnell 17/5/1928, Kempthorne to Morris: Suva 15/2/1928 (NAF/DP/HO III/Correspondence B. Vea 1925-1940). 29 Interviews with Bp. Fine Halapua: Halaleva 16/3/1988, 6/7/1988; F.T. & Herald 4/9/1924, 5/9/1924; letter from Helge Naes (archivist) to writer: Riksarkivet, Oslo 18/1/1988. 30 Interview with Kepueli Komiti: Mo'unga-one 27/7/1988. 31 ACR; various; Notes taken by writer at a faikava: Hihifo, Lifuka 20/7/1988. 32 Lesiseta Pekia - Vava'u *Death Register* (Courthouse, Neiafu); interviews with Palu Fifita Lavulavu & Noamani Liu: Ovaka 6/4/1988, Finau Fatai: St. Andrew's School, Longolongo. 33 Kempthorne to Miss Horne: Suva 12/1/1923 (USPG/MR/1923/A/58); "Report of the Tongan Mission"by Y.S. Mark to 1926 Synod (Standing Committee Minute Book: 50 Diocesan Office, Suva): interview with Lemani Taufa and others: Lape 5/4/1988. 34 Lowe to Pascoe: London 14/6/1921 (USPG/CLR/NZ&P/4/106);. Reports of meetings of the Bishop Willis Memorial Committee: London 3/6/1921, 14/10/1921; Declaration of Trust as to the Nuku'alofa Church Building Fund (NAF/DP/DT/5). 35 Montgomery, H.H. The Problem of Special Mission Funds in relation to the Parent Society 1903. 36 Will of Alfred Willis (Diocesan Office, Suva File TR/2/2/5); "The Willis Wills" courtesy of R. Lowe, Lower Hutt. 37 Kempthorne to Lowe: Suva 12/5/1926; Henry Smith to Kempthorne: Honolulu 3/7/1926; copious correspondence between Lowe, Y.S. Mark, Kempthorne and others (NAF/DP/DT/11); Burial Register, Braceborough (J. Duckett to writer: Langtoft, Peterborough 2/11/1987); A.B.M. Review 12/5/1927: 45. 38 Bp. J.A. La Mothe to Y.S. Mark: Honolulu 26/11/1927 (JBP); Lowe to Kempthorne: St. Albans 5/3/1928 (NAF/DP/DT/11). 39 A.B.M. Review 12/9/1925; Mark 1936: 8-10; interview with Bp. Fine Halapua; Halaleva 16/3/1988. 40 La Mothe to Y.S. Mark: Honolulu 7/5/1928 (JBP); La Mothe to Kempthorne: Honolulu 4/4/1928; Y.S. Mark to Lowe: Nuku'alofa 1/5/1928 (NAF/DP/DT/5); Standing Committee Minute Book: 92 (Diocesan Office, Suva). 41 Mark 1936: 27; interviews with Lone Vea: Kolofo'ou 22/9/1988, Asita Langi: Mangaia 20/9/1988. 42 ACR; Y.S. Mark to Kempthorne: Nuku'alofa 25/6/1928 (NAF/DP/DT/5). 43 R. Hyne to Kempthorne: Nuku'alofa 16/9/1928; Favell to Kempthorne: Nuku'alofa 3/3/1929; Kempthorne to Favell: Suva 21/1/1930 (NAF/DP/DT/11). 44 Kempthorne to Lowe: Suva 6/2/1935 (NAF/DP/DT/11).

# CONCLUSION

# THE WORK OF AN INDIVIDUAL?

*"Of late, a Mission of our Church had been opened in Tonga, but it is as yet in some sense the work of an individual." (Montgomery 1903b:403)*

The establishment of the Anglican Church in Tonga was in many senses the work of an individual. Alfred Willis had gone to Tonga on his own initiative and motivated by a complex interaction of personal, social and religious factors. He had done this without the knowledge or permission of the Bishop of London, into whose jurisdiction, at least in theory he ventured. The Archbishop of Canterbury, to whom Willis was subject as an extra-provincial bishop in Honolulu, had not sanctioned the establishment of a new work or the formation of a Tongan diocese. Willis' intrusion into the Kingdom was also seen as breaking the comity which had existed between the Wesleyans, the London Missionary Society and the Anglicans since at least the 1840s. Such was the situation within the Anglican Church which had prompted Bishop Montgomery's comment in 1903.

Montgomery was unaware how prophetic his words were to be. Like Shirley Baker had been before him, Willis was the sole source of Anglican tradition for his Church in Tonga from his arrival in June 1902 until his departure for England in April 1920. Although he had not made the original translations from the *Book of Common Prayer* into Tongan, he interpreted this Anglican yardstick according to his view of the Church Catholic. In doing so, he had attempted to make considerable changes to the religious customs of the group of Tongans who had called him to the Kingdom. Those who had remained with his Mission, and the few who had joined in later years, were willing to accept these changed religio- cultural circumstances. In addition, due to the virtual absence of hou'eiki in his Church, particularly after the defections of 1904, Willis had become the undisputed temporal leader of his tiny flock, who tended to look to their aged bishop rather than traditional Tongan authority structures as their focus of unity.

Willis had financed his Church from his own private income, the subscriptions of his family and friends in England and America, and after 1908, the small stipend he received from the S.P.G. in recognition of his chaplaincy to the English community in Tonga. All printing, travel and building expenses, with the exception of the construction of the churches at

Mo'unga-one and Lape, plus a substantial portion of Sang Mark's stipend, had come from these sources, over which Willis exercised absolute control.

Sang Mark, a man of considerable natural talents in many areas, would never have ventured to Tonga without Willis' influence. Sang Mark's view of the Church and his aspirations for the Anglican Church in Tonga, were dependent on his elderly patron, in both their origin and exercise. This was demonstrated in Sang Mark's unsuccessful attempts to continue the Tongan Anglican Mission in a similar fashion after 1920, devoid of Willis' leadership, finance or overseas contacts.

Through Willis' persistent presence in the Kingdom, his Tongan Mission had been accepted as a legitimate part of the Anglican Communion, albeit as part of the Diocese of Polynesia. The Tongan membership however, had little concept of being part of a diocesan family. Their view of the wider Church had been interpreted to them by Willis, whose concept of the Church true and Catholic was rooted in the Missionary Bishopric movement and the religious controversies of mid nineteenth century England.

Willis had failed to grasp the imagination of a significant portion of the Tongan population in either rank or number. In this regard, his efforts had much in common with the other second-wave denominations that were established contemporaneously in the Kingdom. He failed to understand that the *sipinga* of lotu Uesiliana was deeply rooted in Tongan society, and that, despite his own view of the superiority of his Catholic Christianity, the bulk of the population saw little reason to change their religious allegiance. It had been a case of 'first come, first served' and the actions of an elderly English bishop, or the vigorous proselytism of the 'sects', would make little difference.

What Willis did provide was an alternative denominational focus for the urbanised Tongan community in Kolofo'ou. By the time that the new 'permanent' St. Paul's Church was built in memory of Willis and consecrated in 1931, this congregation was virtually all that remained of his grandiose scheme to establish the Anglican Church as the National Church of Tonga.

In the decade that had passed since Willis' death, a legend had grown up surrounding his life and work. Nothing was known in Tonga about the controversies surrounding his thirty years in Honolulu. If any in the Kolofo'ou knew of either the standoff between Willis and the English Church authorities, or the defection of Taemanusa and Tevita Ula Afuha'amango in the early years, this was seen to be of little relevance.

What was cherished were the stories of his definite pastoral concern, his efforts to obtain land for his Church, and his attempts to provide a `correct' translation of the Scriptures. Alfred Willis' understanding of the Tongan Prayer Book and Hymns, the seven sacraments and apostolic succession, an elevated view of the priesthood, and the superiority of the Church true and Catholic were the sipinga which they had received from their revered founder. There was no doubt that the tall straight-backed Englishman, with his long white beard and black cassock, had left a definite impression on the members of the Anglican Church in Tonga. This included even those who had been too young to remember him well, or who joined the Church since his death, through St. Andrew's School or the efforts of Willis' prodigy, Sang Mark.

The same conservatising tendency which had been at work in preventing the adoption of new religio-cultural concepts by the bulk of the Tongan population, were later at work within the small Anglican community. Having received from Willis his view what it was to be an Anglican, it was unlikely that they would see any need to change from his sipinga. In addition, the general indifference that was a feature of the inter-Church relationships in Tonga in the period prevented the dissemination of ideas to or from other denominations.

Other factors ensured that Alfred Willis' presence continued to be felt in the Anglican Church in the Kingdom. Tonga was one amongst several isolated parishes within the Diocese of Polynesia. Bishop Lionel Kempthorne and the sole charge priests he appointed following Sang Mark's departure, continued to be the only links with the wider Anglican Church. The European congregation, as in Willis' time, continued to have a high proportion of expatriates, who, it would be thought, potentially provided a source of differing views of Anglicanism. However, in addition to the social norms of Nuku'alofa which encouraged little contact between the two congregations, the majority of short-stay Europeans were not competent speakers of the Tongan language. This was also the case for the series of European priests who headed the Mission and St. Andrew's School, who had made little effort to learn the vernacular. They relied on the Tongan layreaders and teachers for the day to day running of the Tongan services and the school.

Despite promising moves in the mid 1920s, Kempthorne made little further effort to encourage an indigenous ministry in the diocese, including Tonga. Those who had earlier begun training lost heart, and the opportunity to promulgate a different outlook through that avenue was lost. Numbers in the Kolofo'ou congregation grew steadily through the 1930s and 1940s, largely through the success of the school. The outlook, however remained rooted in the Willis era, with a dependency on overseas sources of authority, priesthood and finance. This left the Anglican Church in Tonga with little concept of self-support or financial responsibility, and a view of the priesthood that it was unobtainable by local people. In its encapsulated Tongan form, the outlook of Alfred Willis of the Church true and Catholic, with its origin in the mid nineteenth century was able to survive into the mid twentieth century.

Such was the legacy of Alfred Willis.

# SELECTED BIBLIOGRAPHY

## 1.ALFRED WILLIS AND THE TONGA MISSION PRESS

*Printed material produced by Alfred Willis 1877 to 1926, or attributed to Willis through its publication by the Mission Press. Those marked \* are known only from secondary sources and may no longer be in existence in 1991. Material is arranged chronologically wherever possible.*

Honolulu Diocesan Almanac for 1877 Honolulu: Iolani College 1876
Occasional Paper and Annual Report of the Hawaiian Mission ... 31st December, 1883
London: Hawaiian Mission Assn 1884
Occasional Paper and Annual Report of the Hawaiian Mission ... 31st December, 1884
London: Hawaiian Mission Assn 1885
Occasional Paper and Annual Report of the Hawaiian Mission ... 31st December, 1885
London: Hawaiian Mission Assn 1886
Occasional Paper and Annual Report of the Hawaiian Mission ... 31st December, 1886
London: Hawaiian Mission Assn 1887
Occasional Paper and Annual Report of the Hawaiian Mission ... 31st December, 1887
London: Hawaiian Mission Assn 1888
\*The essential need of unity in the Cathedral Church: or Reasons why the expedient of a dual organisation, permitted in 1885 to meet a temporary emergency, should now be discontuned
Honolulu: R. Ghere Steam Book and Job Printer 1893
Occasional Paper and Annual Report of the Hawaiian Mission ... 31st December, 1892
London: Hawaiian Mission Assn 1893
Letter from the Lord Bishop of Honolulu and Annual Report of the Hawaiian Mission ... 31st
December, 1895 London: Hawaiian Mission Assn 1896
Appeal for the Church in Samoa by the Bishop of Honolulu London: n.p. 1897
Letter from the Lord Bishop of Honolulu and Annual Report of the Hawaiian Mission ... 31st
December, 1897 London: Hawaiian Mission Assn 1898
Address of the Bishop to the Clergy and Laity of the Diocese of Honolulu Honolulu: n.p. 1899
Koe tu'utu'uni koe'uhi koe gahi lotu ki he Bogibogi mo e Efiafi 'oe Sabate Auckland: Mission
Press 1902 *Morning and Evening Prayer*
Ko e Fehui me e Tali - A Catechism Auckland: Mission Press 1902
'Letter of January 17th 1903' [no title] London: n.p. 1903
'Koe Babitaiso Ma'oni' Auckland: Mission Press n.d. [1903?]
*Baptism service first section in untitled pub.*
"The Church in the South Seas" Church Times 19th February, 1904 :248-249
Koe tu'utu'uni koe'uhi koe babitaiso 'ae tamaiki 'i Abi Nuku'alofa: Mission Press [1904?]
*Private baptism of infants in the home*
\*Ko e Konisitutone Nuku'alofa: Mission Press 1904 *Constitution*

*Koe gaahi himi 'oe Jiaji Igilani 'i Toga kuo hiki mei he lea  fakaBilitania Auckland: Mission
Press 1905 *Hymns translated  from English*
"Letter of Bishop Willis and Report of 1904 on the Anglican Church in Tonga" (as reprinted
in Pacific Commercial Advertiser 25th May 1905)
"Constitution and Canons of the Anglican Church in Tonga May 1904. Revised May 1906"
(Typescript copy) 1906
"To All the Supporters of the Anglican Church in Tonga" Nuku'alofa - typescript 11th June 1906
Ko e Konisitutone Nuku'alofa: Mission Press 1906 *Constitution*
*Ko e fonoga ki he goue Fakaofoofa Nuku'alofa: Mission Press
*Bishop Wilberforce's allegory 'The Spring Morning' in Agathis*
*Ko e gahi Same a Tevita Nuku'alofa: Mission Press 1907 *Psalms of David*
Letter of Bishop Willis and Report for 1907 for the Anglican  Church in Tonga
London: Tongan Mission Fund 1908
*Ko e gahi lotu oe Episele mo e gahi Kosibele, ke fai ki he  ta'u Nuku'alofa: Mission Press 1909
*Collects, Epistles and  Gospels for the year*
Letter of Bishop Willis and Report for 1908 for the Anglican  Church in Tonga
London: Tongan Mission Fund 1909
Letter of Bishop Willis and Report for 1910 for the Anglican  Church in Tonga
London: Tongan Mission Fund 1911
Letter of Bishop Willis and Report for 1911 for the Anglican  Church in Tonga
London: Tongan Mission Fund 1912
Letter from Bishop Willis to the Supporters of the Anglican  Church in Tonga
Braceborough: n.p. 1912
Ko e tohi 'oe Gahi Lotu Bogibogi mo Efiafi o fakatatau ki he  tu'utu'uni koe 'uhi koe takga'i 'ae
Feohi'aga Ma'oni'oni ke  fai 'ihe Jiaja[sic] Faka-Igilani 'i Toga (The Book of Common  Prayer
and Hymns- Tonga) London: S.P.C.K. 1912 Reprinted 1938
Mormonism: Whence is it? The True Story of J. Smith and the  Book of Mormon
London: S.P.C.K. 1913
Letter of Bishop Willis and Report for 1913 for the Anglican  Church in Tonga
London: Tongan Mission Fund 1914
Letter of Bishop Willis and Report for 1915 for the Anglican  Church in Tonga
London: Tongan Mission Fund 1916
Anglican Church Accounts for 1915 Nuku'alofa: Anglican Mission Press 1916
The Unity of the Bible Part One London: Nisbet and Co. 1916
A Few Words on the War Nuku'alofa: Anglican Mission Press 1916
Passiontide and Easter - to the members of the Anglican  Church in Tonga
Nuku'alofa: Anglican Mission Press 1916
Anglican Church Accounts for 1916 Nuku'alofa: Anglican Mission Press 1917
"The Seventh Day Adventists" Church Gazette of the Diocese of  Auckland V67 No.9
(1917):180
Resolution touching the Psalter. A letter to ... the Lord  Archbishop of Canterbury D.D. from

the Octagenarian Assistant Bishop for Tonga Nuku'alofa: Anglican Mission Press 1917
A Litany and Hymns for use during the War Nuku'alofa: Anglican Mission Press 1917
Letter of Bishop Willis and Report for 1917 for the Anglican Church in Tonga
London: Tongan Mission Fund 1918
Koe gahi akonaki oe Jiaji ki he Ta'u fakakilisitiane Nuku'alofa: Anglican Mission Press 1918
Anglican Church Accounts for 1917 Nuku'alofa: Anglican Mission Press 1918
Letter of Bishop Willis and Report for 1918 for the Anglican Church in Tonga
London: Tongan Mission Fund 1919
Anglican Church Accounts for 1918 Nuku'alofa: Anglican Mission Press 1919
The Unity of the Bible Part Two (H.B. Simeon ed.) Hythe: W.S. Paine and Co. 1926
Tonga Church Chronicle - Ko e Niusipepa ke fakamatala'ae Gaue 'ae Jiaji Faka Igilani 'i Tonga
(produced quarterly April 1913 to January 1915) Nuku'alofa: Government Printer


*The following material was also produced by the Anglican Mission Press, but is not known to*
*have survived. Correct titles unknown - in Tongan unless specified.*


`Translation of Calendar, Litany and Collects' 1903
`Order for Holy Communion' 1903
`A small catechism on the faith an duty of a Christian' 1905
`A tract on confirmation' 1905?
`Private Prayers for Children' 1905?
`A preparation for Holy Communion and thanksgiving after' 1906?
`A catechism on the Church of England showing that it is not the creation of Henry VIII as the
R.C. priests persist in telling our people' 1906?
`Tract warning of anti-Christian teaching of the Mormon missionaries' 1911 *3000 copies*
`Present day tracts in Tongan 1916-1917 *500 copies of each*
    1) A warning against erroneous teaching
    2) The evidence for the Lord's resurrection Part One
    3) The evidence for the Lord's resurrection Part Two
    4) The Call to Repentance'
`The Holy Communion - why I should receive it' *300 copies*
`Order of confirmation for those who had no godparents - translation from the Prayer Book of
the Church of Scotland' *150 copies*
`The calendar in Tongan and English for 1916 and 1917' *100 copies each year*
`Translation of Father Conrad's Chaplet of Prayer with illustrations' 1918

# 2. REFERENCES GENERAL - PUBLISHED

Annextures to the Report of the High Commissioner to the Western Pacific on the events in the Tonga Islands December 1904 and January 1905 Suva: Government Printer 1905

Baker, Beatrice Shirley and Connel, John V.D. Koe Fonokalafi Auckland: Wilson and Horton 1899

Baker, Lillian and Baker, Beatrice Shirley Memoirs of the Rev. Dr. Shirley Waldemar Baker D.D., L.L.D. Missionary and Prime Minister London: Mayflower Publishing 1951

Baker, Shirley Waldemar An English and Tongan Vocabulary and a Tongan and English Vocabulary with a list of idiomatic phrases and Tongan Grammar Auckland:Wilson and Horton 1897

Baker, Shirley Waldemar (attrib.) Ko e Konifemaiseni pe ko e hilifakinima kiate kinautolu kuo babitaiso Auckland: Wilson And Horton n.d. Confirmation service

Baker, Shirley Waldemar (attrib.) Koe Fehui moe Tala [sic] oe Jiaji Igilani Auckland: Wilson and Horton n.d.A catechism

Baker, Shirley (attrib.) Koe g. lotu ki he Bogobogi moe Efiafi 'oe Sabate Auckland: Wilson and Horton 1900 Morning and evening prayer

Baker, Shirley (attrib.) Tohi Mahina oe Jiaji Igilani o Toga Auckland: Wilson and Horton n.d Calendar

Baker, Shirley (attrib.) Koe tohi 'oku fakaha ai hono fai 'oe Sakalameneti 'ae Ohomohe 'ae 'Eiki Auckland: Wilson and Horton n.d. Holy communion service

Bakker, M.L. A Demographic Analysis of the Population of Tonga 1777-1975 (Occasional Paper No. 14) Noumea: South Pacific Commission 1979

Barnes, W.H. Bishop Willis of Honolulu and Tonga Memorial Fund London: no pub. 1921

Bird, Isabella (Mrs Bishop) Six months in the Sandwich Islands London: John Murray 1874 (1906 reprint)

Brandreth, H.R.T. Episcopi Vagantes and the Anglican Church London: S.P.C.K. 1947

Britsch, R. Lanier Unto the Islands of the Sea Salt Lake City: Deseret Book Co. 1986

Chadwick, Owen The Mind of the Oxford Movement London: Black 1960

Chadwick, Owen The Victorian Church (2 vols) London: Adam, Charles and Black 1966

Clarke, H.L. Constitutional Church Government in the Dominions beyond the seas and in other parts of the Anglican Communion London: S.P.C.K. 1924

Collocott, E.E.V. "Notes on Tongan Religion" Parts I & II Journal of the Polynesian Society V30 (1921) :152-163, 227-240

Correspondence 27th June 1902 to 26th May 1906 relating to affairs in Tonga (Australian No.1 82) London: Colonial Office 1906

Cummins, H.G. (comp.) Sources of Tongan History Vol.1 A collection of documents, extracts, and contemporary opinions in Tongan political history Nuku'alofa: Tupou High School 1972

Cummins, H.G. "Missionary Chieftain - James Egan Moulton and Tongan Society 1965- 1909" (Ph.D. thesis Australian National University, Canberra) 1980

<u>Cyclopedia of Samoa, Tonga, Tahiti and the Cook Islands</u>
Sydney: McCarron, Stewart and Co 1907

Davidson, R. <u>The Five Lambeth Conferences</u> London: S.P.C.K. 1920

Dektor-Korn, S.R. "After the missionaries came; denominational diversity in the Tonga Islands" <u>Mission, Sect and Church in Oceania</u> Monograph No.6 Assn of Social Anthropology in Oceania: 395-422 Ann Arbor: University of Michigan Press 1978

Ellem, Elizabeth Wood "Queen Salote Tupou III and Tungī Mailefihi - a study in leadership in 20th century Tonga" (Ph.D. thesis, University of Melbourne) 1981

Ellem, Elizabeth Wood "Salote of Tonga and the Problem of National Unity" <u>Journal of Pacific History</u> V18 (1983): 163

Evans, J.H. <u>Southern See</u> Dunedin: John McIndoe 1968

Forman, Charles "Tonga's Tortured Venture in Church Unity" <u>Journal of Pacific History</u> v13 (1978):3-21

Forman, Charles <u>The Island Churches of the South Pacific - Emergence in the Twentieth Century</u> (American Society of Missiology Series No.5) Maryknoll N.Y: Orbis Books 1982

Forman, Charles "Playing Catch-up Ball: the history of financial dependence in the Pacific Island Churches" <u>Missions and Missionaries in the Pacific</u> (Char. Miller ed.) New York and Toronto: Edwin Mellan Press 1985

Fusitu'a, 'Eseta Fulivai "King George Tupou II and the Government of Tonga" (M.A. thesis Australian National University, Canberra) 1976

Fusitu'a, 'Eseta Fulivai and Rutherford, Noel "George Tupou II and the British Protectorate" <u>Friendly Islands - a history of Tonga</u> (Rutherford, Noel ed.)
Melbourne: Oxford University Press 1977

Gallagher, Mark "No more a Christian Nation" (Ph.D. thesis University of Hawai'i) 1983

Garrett, John <u>To Live Among The Stars</u> Geneva and Suva: World Council of Churches and Institute of Pacific Studies 1982

Gifford, E.W. "Euro-American Acculturation in Tonga" <u>Journal of the Polynesian Society</u> v33 (1924):281-292

Gifford, E.W. <u>Tongan Society</u> (Bulletin No.61) Honolulu: Bernice B. Bishop Museum 1929

Gunson, Niel "Victorian Christianity in the South Seas - a survey" <u>Journal of Religious History</u> v8 (1974): 183-197

Hands, W.J. <u>Polynesia</u> London: S.P.G. 1929

Heeney, William Brian D. <u>A Different Kind of Gentleman</u> Springfield, Ohio: Archon Books 1976

Hilliard, D. <u>God's Gentlemen - A History of the Melanesian Mission</u>
St Lucia, Qld: University of Queensland 1978

<u>The Honourable R.J. Seddon's Visit to the South Seas</u> Wellington: Government Printer 1900

Hook, Herbert "Christianity in Polynesia with particular reference to the work of the Anglican Church" (B.A. Honours thesis, University of New Zealand, Otago) 1936

Hopkins, Manly <u>Hawai'i; the past, present and future of its Island Kingdom</u> London: Longman, Green and Co. 1862

Howe, K.R. <u>Where the waves fall</u> London: George Allen and Unwin 1984 im Thurn, Sir Everard F. Report on Tongan Affairs Dec 1904 - Jan 1905 Suva: Government Printer 1905

Jay, Elizabeth ed. The Evangelical and Oxford Movements Cambridge: University Press 1983

Kasten, Dennis A. "Nineteenth Century Chinese Christian Missionaries in Hawai'i" Hawaiian Journal of History v12 (1978):61ff

Laracy, Hugh "The Catholic Mission" Friendly Islands - a history of Tonga (Rutherford, Noel ed.) Melbourne: Oxford University Press 1977

Lātūkefu, Sione "Oral Traditions - an appraisal of their value in historical research in Tonga" Journal of Pacific History V3 (1968):135- 143

Lātūkefu, Sione Church and State in Tonga Canberra: Australian National University 1974

Lātūkefu, Sione The Tonga Constitution - a brief history to celebrate its centenary Nuku'alofa: Tonga Traditions Committee 1975

Lavaka, Penelope A. "The Limits of Advice: Britain and the Kingdom of Tonga 1900-1970" (Ph.D . thesis Australian National University) 1981

Ledyard, Patricia 'Utulei, my Tongan home London: Robert Hale and Co. 1974

Liliuokalani Hawaii's Story by Hawaii's Queen Boston: Lothrop, Leo and Shepherd Co. 1898

Lowe, Robert "The Willis Wills"(photocopied for private circulation) 1990

Mark, Yim Sang Bishop Willis Memorial Church in Tonga Completed Honolulu: n.p. 1931

Mark, Yim Sang St Peter's Church ... An Historical Account of the First Chinese Episcopal Church in Hawai'i Honolulu: W.W. Ahana 1936

Mark, Yim Sang "Biographical Notes - address given by Canon Mark at the celebration of his fifty years in the priesthood held at St John's Church, Los Angeles: mimeographed 1960

Mark, Yim Sang "A brief story of my life" Los Angeles: mimeographed 1964

Methodist Church in Australasia - Report of the First General Conference Melbourne: Methodist Church 1904

Mission and Ministry - Diocese of Polynesia Synod 1966 Taronaniara, Solomon Islands: Diocese of Melanesia Press 1966

Montgomery, H.H. The Problem of Special Mission Funds in relation to the Parent Society London: S.P.G. 1903

Montgomery, H.H. "The Anglican Church in the Pacific" East and West V1, No.4 (1903):402-412

Moulton, J.E. Moulton of Tonga London: Epworth 1921

Muir, Andrew Forest "Ordinations by the Bishops of Honolulu 1862-1902" Historical Magazine of the Protestant Episcopal Church V20 (1951):328-331

McArthur, Norma Island Populations of the Pacific Canberra: Australian University Press 1967

McCall, T.B. "Report of the Home Secretary ... to the Chairman of the Australian Board of Missions May June 1958" Sydney - mimeographed 1958

Neill, J.S. Ten Years in Tonga London: Hutchison 1955

Nevill, E.R. A Bishop's Diary: Samuel Tarrant Nevill Dunedin: Otago Daily Times 1922

Old, Brian M. "A History of St Stephen's School 1844-1974" (M.A. thesis University of Auckland) 1974

Pascoe, C.F. Two Hundred Years of the S.P.G. 1701-1901 London: S.P.G. 1901

Pinson, W.J. "The Diocese of Polynesia 1868-1910" (B.D. thesis Pacific Theological College) 1970

Restarick, Henry Bond Hawai'i 1778-1920 from the Standpoint of a Bishop Honolulu: Paradise of the Pacific 1924

Ross, Angus New Zealand Aspirations in the Pacific in the 19th Century London: Clarendon Press 1964

Rutherford, Noel Shirley Baker and the King of Tonga Melbourne: Oxford University Press 1971

Scarr, Deryck Fragments of Empire - a history of the Western Pacific High Commission 1877-1914 Canberra: Australian National University Press 1967

Servante, Arthur W. "South Sea Paradise" The Listener V20 No.507(1938):643-645

Stanton, G.N. "The Bishop of Dunedin, the Anglican Church and Polynesia" (B.A. Honours thesis University of Otago) 1961

Steley, Dennis "Advances and Reversals in Polynesia 1890- 1918" Symposium on Adventist History in the South Pacific 1885-1918 (Ferch, Arthur J ed.) Wahroonga, N.S.W.: South Pacific Division of Seventh Day Adventist 1986

Strong, E.H. The Mission in Tonga Nuku'alofa: Mission Press 1921

Sullivan, Martin Watch How You Go London: Hodder and Stoughton 1975

Suter, Andrew Burn Report of the Right Reverend Andrew Burn Suter D.D. Bishop fo Nelson to the Most Reverend the Primate of the Church of the Province of New Zealand on his Lordship's Visit to Samoa and Fiji Christchurch: Angus Turner 1886

Teale, Ruth "Dr. Pusey and the Church Overseas" Pusey Rediscovered Butler, Perry ed. London: S.P.C.K. 1983

Thompson, H.P. Into All Lands - a history of the S.P.G. 1701- 1951 London: S.P.C.K. 1951

Thomson, Basil Savage Island - an account of a sojourn in Niue and Tonga London: John Murray 1902

Thomson, Basil The Scene Changes New York: Doubleday 1937

Tohi, Viliami Tavake "A Study in the nature of the Church as seen in the Anglican Church in Tonga" (B.D. thesis Pacific Theological College) 1972

Tongan Law Reports Vol.II Nuku'alofa: Government Printer 1963

Trood, Thomas Island Remininsences - a graphic detailed account of a life spent in the South Sea Islands Sydney: McCarron, Stewart and Co. 1912

Tu'ivakanō, Kilisitina "Notes on the History of the Anglican Church in Tonga - in Tongan and English for Bishop J.C. Vockler" Nuku'alofa typescript n.d.

Whelan, John "The Anglican Church in Korea" International Review of Missions V49 No.194 (1960):157-166

White, James F. The Cambridge Movement - the Ecclesiological Society and the Gothic Revival Cambridge: University Press 1962

Whonsbon-Aston, C.W. Pacific Irishman Sydney: Australian Board of Missions 1970

Williams, H.W. and Simkin, W.J. The Dioceses of New Zealand and Associated Missions Wellington: Church of the Province of New Zealand 1934

Wood, A.H. "The Present Situation in Tonga" Australian Methodist Missionary Review
V36 No.1 (1926):5-8
Wood, A.H. History and Geography of Tonga Nuku'alofa: Government Printer 1932
Wood, A.H. Overseas Missions of the Australian Methodist Church Vol.1 Tonga and Samoa
Melbourne: Aldersgate Press 1975
Wood, A.H. and Ellem, E.W. "Queen Salote Tupou III" Friendly Islands - a history of Tonga
(Rutherford, Noel ed.) Melbourne: Oxford University Press 1977


# 3. MANUSCRIPT AND ARCHIVES REFERENCES


## UNITED KINGDOM
**Archives of the United Society for the Propagation of the Gospel, Rhodes House, Oxford (USPG).**
Consulted on microfilm (A.J.C.P - M series) Extensive use of material concerning the Society
for the Propagation of the Gospel in Foreign Parts, including copies of letters sent, copies of
letters recieved, originals of letters received, missionary reports, ledgers, and some printed
material.Extracts used with permission of the archivist, Mrs Catherine Wakeling.

**Lambeth Palace Library, London (LPL).**
Consulted on microfilm (A.J.C.P.- M series) Tait Papers volumes 178 & 186
Notes taken on the writer's behalf by Dr. A. Davidson & Ms. A. Denton (Davidson Papers
volume 430, and Fulham Papers - Winningham-Ingram: Willis 1901-1906)

**Public Records Office, London (PRO).**
1851 Census held on microfilm

**Wiltshire Records Office, Trowbridge (WRO).**
Wells Theological Records 2308/WTC - in correspondence with the archivist, K.H. Rogers.

## FIJI
**Records of the Diocese of Polynesia, National Archives of Fiji, Suva (NAF/DP).**
Tonga Parochial District DT files containing incomplete collection of correspondence between
Willis, Baker and others, some printed material, and correspondence relating to the building of
St Paul's Church, Nuku'alofa. Head office correspondence files also consulted (HO III).

**Bishop Jabez Bryce Papers (JBP)**
Private collection of original private and official correspodence of Willis, Baker, William Lowe
and others dating from 1872. Contains licences of Alfred Willis, drafts of letters, some printed

material, and original sermon notes

**Diocesan Office, Suva.**
Records of Standing Committee and Synods.
Correspondence relating to Bishop Willis endowment of an Eastern Polynesian diocese
TR/2/2/5. All used with the permission of Bishop Jabez Bryce.

# TONGA
**Anglican Church Register, St Paul's Church, Nukualofa (ACR).**
Probably only surviving register from the period of Alfred Willis and Y.S. Mark. Contains
register of baptisms, receptions, confirmations and funerals, including those conducted by Rev'd
William Horsfall 1896-1898. Used by permission of Fr. Mataiasi 'Ahokava.

**Free Wesleyan Church Records, Nuku'alofa, Pangai and Neiafu.**
Baptism and marriage records, including some registers of the Free Church 1885-1924.
Minutes of the annual conferences of the Free Church (in Tongan) consulted on microfilm
(P.M.B.979)

**Registers of Births, Deaths and Marriages held at the Courthouses, Nuku'alofa, Pangai and
Neiafu.** Used in the original

# NEW ZEALAND
**Customs Records, National Archives of New Zealand, Auckland and Wellington
(NANZ/C).**
Shipping registers, correspondence registers and original correspondence relating to Y.S. Mark's
entry to New Zealand in 1910.

**St Stephen's School Records, Education Department Records, National Archives of New
Zealand, Auckland (NANZ/BAAA).**
Relating to Tongan students at the school 1915-1930s

**Samoan Archives, National Archives of New Zealand, Wellington (NANZ/Samoan
Archives/BCS).**
Diaries and correspondence of Thomas Trood, Acting British Vice Consul in Apia 1900-1916.

**Bank of New Zealand Archives, Wellington**
Papers relating to S.W. Baker's involvement, in correspondence with the archivist, R.H.Griffen.

**St Mary's Church Archives, New Plymouth.**
Papers relating to E.H. Strong, in correspondence with the archivist, Mrs M. McConachie.

# UNITED STATES OF AMERICA

**Papers of Helen Fahnestock Campbell.**

Diaries, notes and photographs of the visit of Clarence Gordon Campbell and Helen Fahnestock Campbell to Tonga in 1902 and 1903. Extracts used by permission of Clarence F. Michalis, their grandson, New York.

**Records of the Episcopal Church in Hawai'i**

Printed material, newspaper clippings etc, used in correspondence with the archivist, Fr. Kenneth Perkins, Honolulu.

**Notes of oral research conducted by the writer in New Zealand and Tonga 1987- 1989. Referenced in source notes.**

# INDEX

Selwyn, G.A. Bishop 9 ,25 ,29, 82
Selwyn compact 29 ,82
Seventh Day Adventists 19, 64 ,69
Siaine 40 ,45 ,52
Siasi 'a Vika 2 ,13
Siasi Tau'ataina 11 ,37 ,42 ,54 ,64 ,94 ,101
Simeon, G.B. Rev'd 27 ,56
St Andrew's School 55 ,60 ,64 ,94 ,100 ,104 ,105 ,108
St Mary's Girls' Hostel 108
St Peter's Chinese Church, Honolulu 56 ,107
St Stephen's School, Auckland 65, 105
Staley, T.N. Bishop 20 ,24
Strong, E.H. Rev'd 97-99
Suter, A.N. Bishop 10
T
Taemanusa 40 ,46 ,57 ,58 ,79
Talo, Isileli 39 ,65
Taufa, Sione 39 ,46 ,64
Taufa, Sulio 19 ,40 ,46 ,58
Terapo, Harry 86
Thomson, Basil 75 ,76 ,77 ,89
Tonga Church Chronicle 56
Tongan layreaders 46 ,51 ,96
Tongan Mission Fund 106
Trood, Thomas 10 ,31 ,49 ,50
Tu'itavake, Nelson 94 ,102
Tu'ivakano, Kilisitina 40 ,46 ,79 ,80
Tu'ivakano, Tevita Polutele Kaho 19 ,36 ,40 ,57 ,59 ,77, 78 ,90 ,99
Tuku'aho 13
Tulimafua, Talaiasi 39 ,46 ,60 ,63
Tungi 14-40
Tupou College 39
Twitchell, Bishop 62, 85, 89, 97, 99
V
Vava'u, Anglican Church in 46 ,53, 65
Vava'u, Anglican Church in after 1920 104
Vea, Filipe 40 ,46 ,50 ,51 ,60 ,63
Vea, Lesieli 40 ,60
Vea, Paula 98 ,102 ,103

Vea, Tevita 60
W
Wallace, G. Rev'd 25
Watkin, Jabez Rev'd 12, 16, 42 ,70 ,81 ,87 ,94 ,100, 101
Wesleyan Mission, relationships with 81, 101
Wesleyan missionaries 9
**Willis, Alfred Bishop**
*in England and Hawai'i*
..family background 20, 23
..theological education 23
..disputes in Honolulu 25
..education in Honolulu 27
..arrival in Honolulu 24
..marriage to Emma Mary Simeon 27
..church in Samoa 30
*in Tonga*
..involvement with Baker 14, 16, 32
..death 96
..Bible translation in Tongan 47 ,94, 96
..church building in Tonga 53
..church organisation in Tonga 51
..control of finances 51 ,56 ,95
..education in Tonga 53 ,54
..first visit to Tonga 10
..involvement with Baker 32
..land acquisition in Tonga 52 ,53, 78
..'permanent church' 94 ,95, 96, 10
..publications 55 ,56 ,89 ,94, 96
*see also Bibliography*
..relationship with Latter Day Saints 28, 69
..Tongan Royal family 34 ,35 , 70, 71 ,77, 81
..worship and practice 45 ,46
Willis, Emma Mary Simeon 27 ,62 ,84 ,96
Willis sisters 109